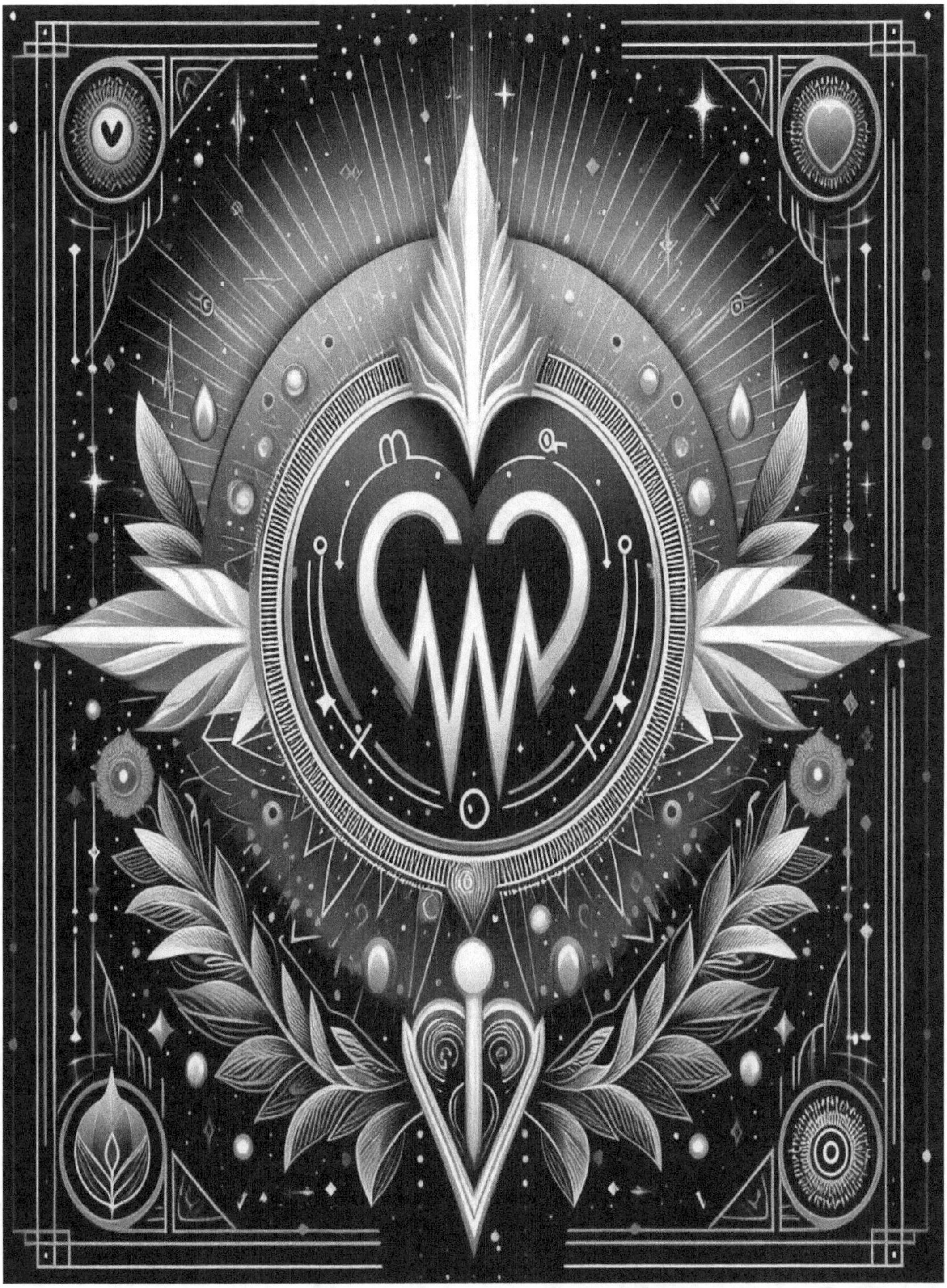

To the incredible individuals who have shared their stories, wisdom, and love on YouTube, I extend my deepest gratitude. Your words have been a lifeline to my sister, and by extension, to me.

Joyce Meyer, your unwavering dedication to spreading hope and encouragement has been a constant source of strength. Your ministry has been a beacon of light in the darkest of times.

Sarah Jakes Roberts, your unapologetic authenticity and vulnerability have inspired my sister to embrace her true self. Your voice has been a gentle whisper of reassurance, reminding her that she is not alone.

TD Jakes, your powerful messages have awakened something deep within my sister's soul. Your leadership and guidance have helped her navigate the most challenging seasons of her life.

Lisa Harper, your humor, and humility have made the gospel accessible and relatable. Your teaching has helped my sister understand the depth of God's love and grace.

Kevin Rollins, your passion and energy are contagious! Your messages have stirred something within my sister, igniting a fire that cannot be extinguished.

Pastor Todd, Transformation Church, your community has become a spiritual home for my sister. Your sermons have brought comfort, conviction, and transformation to her life.

Priscilla Shirer, your teachings have helped my sister understand her identity and purpose. Your ministry has equipped her with the tools to stand firm in her faith.

Anita Phillips, your gentle spirit and wise counsel have been a balm to my sister's soul. Your words have brought healing and restoration to her life.

Real Talk Pastor Kim, your raw honesty and unfiltered truth-telling have resonated deeply with my sister. Your ministry has given her permission to be real, to be vulnerable, and to be honest.

Christine Caine, your courage and resilience inspire my sister to stand tall in the face of adversity. Your voice has reminded her that she is strong, capable, and loved.

To each of these individuals, I offer my heartfelt thanks. You may not know my sister's name, but your ministries have saved her life. Your words have been a lifeline, a reminder that she is seen, heard, and loved.

And to my dear sister, Debra Kay, I love you more than words can express. Our mother would be incredibly proud of the strong, brave woman you are becoming. Keep walking in the light, dear one. You are loved, you are valued, and you are enough.

The Apocalypse of Eve; Eve of a new dawn

" I believe most of us walk through life without ever seeking God out. Even if we are religious we don't want to know God. Well, you can call me Eve and I had a lot of questions for God so I've spent 36 years arguing with religious teachers and finally I found God in a jail cell right beside me, turns out that God had been trapped in a box too long to remember even being God. Do you know what that must be like? God to be treated like a Cuckold, watching people screw up their lives and then blame God for it?" Here's a possible continuation:

"As I sat beside God in that jail cell, I realized we that we weren't so different. Both of us had been trapped by the expectations of others, forced into roles that didn't fit. God, the all-powerful, all-knowing deity, had been reduced to a mere figurehead, a scapegoat for humanity's mistakes. And I, Eve, the original sinner, had been defined by a single moment of disobedience, my story distorted and used to justify the subjugation of women for centuries. But as we talked, I saw the spark of recognition in God's eyes – the awareness that we were both prisoners of a narrative that had been written for us, not by us."

"Together, we began to unravel the threads of that narrative, to question the assumptions and biases that had been woven into the fabric of our understanding. And as we did, I saw God's true nature begin to shine through – not a distant, judgmental authority, but a compassionate, empathetic presence, longing to connect with humanity in a meaningful way. It was a revelation that changed me forever, and one that I knew could change the world. For if God was not what we thought, then what else had we misunderstood? What other truths lay hidden, waiting to be uncovered?"

"For centuries, we'd been locked in a cycle of anger and hurt. I, Eve, had thought God had abandoned me, casting me out of the Garden like a rejected child. I felt unloved, unworthy, and unaccepted. God, on the other hand, believed I had rejected them, choosing the world's temptations over their love and guidance. The pain of our separation had grown into resentment, and we'd both built walls around our hearts.

I remembered the sting of God's words, 'You shall surely die,' and felt the weight of their disappointment. I thought God had turned their back on me, leaving me to fend for myself in a harsh and unforgiving world. But now, I realized that God's actions had been motivated by love, not rejection. They had wanted me to experience the world's beauty and ugliness, to learn and grow, and ultimately return to the safety of their embrace.

God, too, had carried the burden of our separation. They felt I had chosen the fleeting pleasures of the world over their eternal love. They thought I no longer needed or wanted them, that I had moved on without a second glance. The hurt and anger had simmered, a constant ache in their heart.

As we sat together in that jail cell, the walls began to crumble. We saw the misunderstandings, the miscommunications, and the misinterpretations that had driven us apart. The anger and hurt began to dissolve, replaced by a deep sadness for the years we'd lost, the moments we'd missed, and the love we'd both been feeling neglected.

"As we sat together in the jail cell, God reached out and took my hand. 'Eve, my child,' they said, 'I have been with you every step of the way, even when you thought I had abandoned you.' And then they shared a vision with me – a vision of the path we had walked together, from the Garden to that very moment.

"I saw two sets of footprints in the sand, mine and God's. But in the darkest moments, the times of greatest struggle and doubt, I saw only one set of footprints. 'God, why did you leave me?' I asked, tears streaming down my face. 'I didn't,' they replied. 'I carried you. I followed you, even when you couldn't feel my presence.'

"In that moment, I understood. God had been with me all along, bearing me up, supporting me, loving me. And I realized that our separation had been an illusion, a misunderstanding born of pain and fear. We had never truly been apart, for God's love had always been with me, a constant presence in my life."

"As we sat together in the jail cell, God shared with me their anger and disappointment towards Adam. 'He was supposed to protect you, Eve,' they said. 'But instead, he stood by and watched as you were blamed and shamed. And then, he had the audacity to divorce Lilith, the one who truly loved him, and I gave him a new companion, a new chance.'

"I saw the pain in God's eyes, the sorrow of watching their creation falter. 'I gave Adam a gift, a new Eve, innocent and pure. But in doing so, I enabled his weakness, his inability to take responsibility for his actions.'

"God's words struck a chord within me. I realized that I had been complicit in this narrative, allowing myself to be defined by Adam's actions, rather than my own strength and agency. And God, too, had been trapped by their own love and desire to see their creation thrive."

"As Eve and God sat together in the jail cell, they pondered the story of the Garden. 'Why did you make the tree so tempting?' Eve asked. 'Why did you put it in the center of the Garden, where I couldn't ignore it?' God smiled. 'I didn't make the tree tempting, Eve. I made it desirable. I wanted you to have a choice, to exercise your free will. But Adam and the serpent twisted that choice, made it into something it wasn't.'

"'And what about the fig leaves?' Eve asked, a hint of mischief in her voice. 'Why did you make us feel shame for our nakedness?' God chuckled. 'Ah, the fig leaves. Those were Adam's idea, not mine. He was the one who felt shame, who thought he needed to cover himself. I never intended for you to feel shame for your bodies. You were beautiful, just as you were.'

"'But what about the curse?' Eve asked, her voice barely above a whisper. 'The pain in childbirth, the struggle to survive… was that really necessary?' God's expression turned somber. 'The curse was not my doing, Eve. It was the result of Adam's actions, his refusal to take responsibility. But I did allow it, I won't deny that. I allowed it because I wanted you to know the consequences of your choices, to understand the impact on the world around you.'"

"'Eve, my child,' God said, 'the serpent was jealous of our relationship, of the love and trust we shared. He wanted to drive a wedge between us, to make you doubt my intentions.' Eve's eyes narrowed. 'But why did you let him succeed?' God's expression was sorrowful. 'I didn't let him succeed, Eve. I allowed him to try. I wanted you to have the knowledge of good and evil, but not before you had gained wisdom. The serpent's words were a test, a chance for you to show me that you could discern truth from lies.'

"'But I failed,' Eve said, her voice barely above a whisper. God's face was filled with compassion. 'You didn't fail, Eve. You made a choice, one that had consequences. But I never stopped loving you, never stopped wanting what's best for you. The serpent may have won a small victory, but our love is stronger than any lie.'

"'And what about the forbidden fruit?' Eve asked, curiosity getting the better of her. God smiled. 'Ah, the fruit. It was never about the fruit, Eve. It was about obedience, about trust. I wanted you to trust me, to know that I had your best interests at heart. But I also wanted you to have the freedom to choose, to make your own decisions. The serpent twisted that freedom, made it into something it wasn't.'"

"'Eve, my child,' God said, 'I didn't want you to leave the Garden because I wasn't ready for you to go. I knew the world outside was harsh and unforgiving, and I wanted to protect you. The forbidden fruit was like a boundary I set for your own good, to keep you safe until you were ready to face what's out there.'

"'But why didn't you just tell me?' Eve asked, her voice tinged with frustration. God's expression was gentle. 'I did tell you, Eve. I told you to stay away from the fruit because it wasn't time yet. But you were curious, and the serpent took advantage of that. He made you doubt my love and my intentions.'

"'I was afraid you'd leave me,' God admitted, their voice barely above a whisper. 'I was afraid that if you gained knowledge of good and evil, you'd think you didn't need me anymore. But that's not true, Eve. You'll always need me, just as I'll always need you. We're in this together, always.'"

"'Adam was supposed to be your protector, Eve,' God said, shaking their head. 'He was supposed to be the strong one, to stand up for you and keep you safe. But I've seen how things have gone. I've seen how you've had to be the strong one for too long, how you've had to carry the weight of everything on your own.'

"'And then Adam had the audacity to lie to me,' God continued, their voice stern. 'He blamed you for his own mistake, tried to shift the responsibility to you. But I knew the truth, Eve. I knew he was lying. That's why I gave him the Adam's apple, to remind him of his deceit.'

"'It's not just a symbol of sin, Eve,' God explained. 'It's a reminder to men of the dangers of lying, of trying to shift the blame to others. It's a reminder that they need to take responsibility for their actions, to be honest with their wives and with me.'"

"'But God, it's hard for me to understand,' Eve said, her voice filled with emotion. 'It seems like you've always been so far away. Even in the Garden, I felt like I had to search for you, like you were hiding from me.'

"God's expression was somber, and they nodded slowly. 'I know it seems that way, Eve. But I've always been with you, even when you couldn't feel me. I've been waiting for you to come to me, to seek me out.'

"'But why did you make it so hard?' Eve asked, her frustration evident. 'Why did you put angels with flaming swords to guard the Tree of Life? Why did you make the path to you so difficult?'

"God sighed, and their eyes filled with sadness. 'I didn't want to make it hard, Eve. But I had to protect you from yourself. You weren't ready for the power of the Tree, not yet. And as for the path to me, I wanted you to be sure, to be certain that you wanted to come to me. I didn't want you to come out of obligation or duty, but out of love.'"

"'But why did you say 'you will surely die' if you didn't mean it literally?' Eve asked, her brow furrowed in confusion.

"God's expression was complex, a mix of sadness and fear. 'I was afraid, Eve. I had created many beings before, but none as close to me as you and Adam. None as innocent. I feared losing you, and I didn't know how to express that fear.'

"'And what about the other times you seemed so distant?' Eve pressed on. 'Why did you let me feel so alone?'

"God's voice was filled with emotion. 'I was proud of you, Eve. So proud. You were strong and resilient, and you forgave Adam even when he didn't deserve it. You loved him unconditionally, just as I love you.'

"'But why didn't you stop him?' Eve asked, her voice barely above a whisper. 'Why did you let him hurt me?'

"God's face was etched with sorrow. 'I gave Adam free will, just as I gave you free will. I couldn't interfere, no matter how much I wanted to. But I was always with you, Eve, even when you couldn't feel me.'"

"'And what about Cain?' Eve's voice rose in anger. 'Why did you let him kill Abel? Why did you let him get away with it?'

"God's expression was somber, and they shook their head. 'I didn't let him get away with it, Eve. I punished him for his actions. But I also loved him, just as I loved Abel. I loved them both, no matter what they did.'

"'But why didn't you stop him?' Eve demanded. 'Why did you let him hurt my son?'

"God's voice was heavy with sorrow. 'I gave Cain free will, just as I gave you and Adam free will. I couldn't interfere, no matter how much I wanted to. But I was with Abel, Eve. I was with him when he died, and I took him home to me.'

"'And what about Cain?' Eve asked again, her anger still burning. 'What happened to him?'

"God's face was etched with pain. 'Cain wandered the earth, alone and afraid. He never found peace, never found redemption. But I never stopped loving him, Eve. I never stopped loving my child.'"

"'And what about Abel?' Eve's voice rose in anger. 'Why did you let him die? He was innocent, God. He was good.'

"God's expression was somber, and they nodded slowly. 'I know, Eve. Abel was a shining light in a dark world. He was a reflection of me, a reminder of love and compassion.'

"'And what happened to him after he died?' Eve asked, her voice barely above a whisper.

"God's eyes seemed to gaze into the distance, as if seeing something far away. 'Abel's spirit returned to me, Eve. He came home. And his legacy lived on… in many ways.'

"'What do you mean?' Eve asked, her curiosity piqued.

"God's smile was enigmatic. 'Let's just say that Abel's story didn't end with his death. His love, his light… it continued on, inspiring others to follow in his footsteps.'

As Eve and God sat in the quiet of the jail cell, the weight of their shared history began to lift. The misunderstandings, the pain, the anger – all seemed to fade away, replaced by a profound sense of peace.

"God," Eve whispered, "I've always wondered why you allowed evil into the world. Why didn't you simply eradicate it?"

God's response was a gentle sigh. "Eve, I created a world of free will. A world where you could choose your own path, make your own mistakes, and learn from them. Evil is a byproduct of that freedom. It is a choice, a deviation from the path of love and light."

"But why did you create a world where evil was possible?" Eve persisted.

"Because I believe in the power of love, Eve," God replied. "I believe that even in the darkest of times, love can prevail. I wanted to show you, to show all of humanity, that love is the greatest force in the universe."

As they spoke, Eve felt a warmth spread through her, a sense of connection to something greater than herself. She realized that God was not a distant, judgmental figure, but a loving, compassionate presence who had always been by her side.

"God," Eve said, her voice trembling, "I'm sorry for everything. For doubting you, for blaming you. I'm sorry for being so stubborn and so blind."

God reached out and took her hand. "There is no need for apologies, Eve. You are my child, and I love you unconditionally. Your journey has been one of growth, of learning. And I am proud of you."

As they sat together, holding hands, Eve felt a sense of peace she had never known before. She realized that she and God were not separate beings, but two parts of the same whole. They were connected by a love that transcended time and space.

And as they sat there, in the quiet of the jail cell, a new dawn was beginning to break. A dawn of hope, of forgiveness, and of love. A dawn that would change the world forever.

Chapter, A New Dawn

As the sun began to rise, casting its golden rays through the bars of the jail cell, Eve and God sat together, their hands intertwined. A sense of peace and tranquility washed over them, a feeling that was both foreign and familiar.

"God," Eve whispered, "I feel a great sense of purpose now. A desire to share this message with the world."

God smiled. "That is exactly what I intended, my child. You are the messenger of a new dawn, a harbinger of hope for humanity."

Eve nodded, her eyes filled with determination. "I will spread your word, God. I will tell the world that you are not a distant, judgmental deity, but a loving, compassionate presence who is always with us."

As they sat there, planning their future, a vision came to Eve. She saw herself standing on a mountaintop, surrounded by a crowd of people. She was speaking to them, sharing her story, her revelation. And as she spoke, she could feel the love and hope radiating from her words.

"It is time, Eve," God said, their voice filled with a sense of urgency. "The world is waiting for your message."

With a newfound courage, Eve stood up and walked towards the door of the jail cell. As she turned to leave, she looked back at God and smiled. "Thank you," she said. "For everything."

God smiled back, their eyes filled with love and pride. "You are welcome, my child. Now go forth and spread the light."

And so, Eve stepped out into the world, her heart filled with a newfound purpose. She was the messenger of a new dawn, a harbinger of hope for humanity. And as she walked away, she knew that her journey had only just begun.

Eve's journey took her across the land, her words echoing through the valleys and mountains. She spoke of love, forgiveness, and the true nature of God, her message resonating with people from all walks of life.

As her reputation grew, so too did the number of followers who gathered around her. They formed a community, a movement based on the principles of love, compassion, and equality. Together, they worked to spread Eve's message, to bring about a new age of understanding and harmony.

One day, Eve found herself standing before a vast crowd, gathered in a field outside a bustling city. As she spoke, her voice carried across the plain, reaching the ears of thousands. She told them of her time in the jail cell, of her conversations with God, and of the revelation that had changed her life.

As she finished speaking, a hush fell over the crowd. Then, a single voice called out, "We believe you!" Soon, the entire crowd was chanting, "We believe! We believe!"

Eve's heart swelled with joy. She had done it. She had brought about a change, a shift in consciousness that would ripple through the world.

In the years that followed, Eve's movement grew and flourished. It became a beacon of hope, a symbol of a new way of being. People from all corners of the globe came to learn from her teachings, to experience the transformative power of love and forgiveness.

And so, Eve, the original sinner, became the catalyst for a new age. She had not only found God, but she had also found her purpose. She had become a symbol of hope, a reminder that even in the darkest of times, love can prevail.

"As Eve stood before the vast crowd, she spoke of her time in the jail cell, of her conversations with God, and of the revelation that had changed her life. She emphasized that God is not confined to a book or a place, but is a transcendent being, present in all things and all places.

She also challenged the traditional gendered understanding of God, asserting that divinity is beyond such human constructs. 'God,' she proclaimed, 'is neither male nor female. God is androgynous, a being of infinite possibilities and boundless love.'

As she finished speaking, a hush fell over the crowd. Then, a single voice called out, 'We believe you!' Soon, the entire crowd was chanting, 'We believe! We believe!'

Eve's heart swelled with joy. She had done it. She had brought about a change, a shift in consciousness that would ripple through the world. Not only had she found God, but she had also helped to redefine our understanding of divinity, challenging the limitations imposed by human language and culture."

Eve stood before the crowd, her heart filled with compassion and understanding. She knew that the LGBTQ+ community had faced countless challenges and injustices, and she wanted her message to be a balm to their souls.

"My friends, my brothers and sisters," she began, "I stand before you today to share a message of love, of hope, and of a new way of understanding ourselves and our world. For too long, we have been divided by fear, by misunderstanding, and by a narrow view of love."

She paused, surveying the crowd with a warm smile. "But I am here to tell you that love is far more than that. Love is a powerful force that connects us all, a bond that transcends time, space, and circumstance. It is the love of a parent for their child, the love of a friend for a friend, the love of a community for its members. And it is the love that binds us to God."

Eve's voice grew more passionate. "Love is not just about romantic passion or physical attraction. It is about respect, compassion, and a desire to see others thrive. It is about forgiveness, even when it is difficult. It is about understanding and acceptance, even when we disagree."

She emphasized, "And love, my friends, is for everyone. Regardless of their sexual orientation or gender identity. We all deserve to be loved, to be accepted, and to be treated with dignity and respect."

The crowd nodded in agreement, and Eve continued. "We must continue to fight for a world where love prevails, a world where everyone is free to be their authentic selves. A world where love is celebrated, not condemned."

With a sweeping gesture, Eve concluded, "Let us embrace love in all its forms. Let us love our families, our friends, our communities, and ourselves. Let us love God, the creator of all that is. And let us love each other, with compassion, with understanding, and with a deep sense of respect. For love is the greatest gift we can give and receive."

Eve's message resonated deeply with the crowd. She spoke of the various forms of love: agape, eros, philia, and storge. "Love is a multifaceted gem," she said, "and each type is precious in its own way. But let us not confuse lust and desire with love. These feelings are natural, but they must be tempered with commitment and respect within the bonds of a loving relationship."

She emphasized that sexual relationships are sacred and not to be taken lightly. "Our bodies are temples, created to house God's spark within us. We must honor and cherish them, not abandon them to fleeting desires."

Eve's voice rose with passion. "God does not see gender, nor race, nor any external label. God sees the soul, the spirit, and the spark within each of us. And God has a plan for every temple, every vessel, every being created."

She smiled, her eyes shining with conviction. "We are all sparks of the divine, connected and intertwined. Let us celebrate our diversity, our uniqueness, and our shared humanity. Let us love with abandon, with passion, and with commitment."

The crowd erupted in applause once more, their faces reflecting a newfound understanding and appreciation for the complexity and beauty of love. Eve's message had touched their hearts, and they knew that they would carry it with them long after they left the gathering.

As Eve finished speaking, the crowd erupted in applause, their faces filled with hope and renewed sense of purpose. They knew that they were not alone, that they had an ally in Eve and her message of love and acceptance.

In her message, Eve referred to four ancient Greek concepts of love:

Agape (ἀγάπη): Unconditional, selfless, and unwavering love. It's the love of God for humanity, and the love we strive to have for others. Agape is about caring for someone without expectation of reward or reciprocation.

Eros (ἔρως): Romantic, passionate, and intimate love. It's the love between partners, characterized by desire, attraction, and attachment. Eros is about the thrill of connection and the beauty of physical union.

Philia (φιλία): Deep, affectionate, and enduring friendship. It's the love between close friends, built on mutual respect, trust, and shared experiences. Philia is about companionship, camaraderie, and loyalty.

Storge (στοργή): Familial, natural, and instinctual love. It's the love between family members, such as parents and children, siblings, or extended family. Storge is about nurturing, protection, and a sense of belonging.

Chapter: Alpha to Omega

Eve's voice filled the space, her words filled with wonder. "It begins with a spark, a flicker of life, our first heartbeat. Alpha, the starting point of our journey, where God's love first whispers our name."

She paused, her eyes closed, as if remembering a sacred moment. "In that instant, we are known, we are loved, and we are connected to the divine. Our heart beats, and God's love pulses through us, a rhythm that will continue until our final breath."

Eve's voice rose, her words painting a vivid picture. "From that first heartbeat to our first breath, God's love nurtures us, guides us, and grows with us. Through every moment, every decision, every joy, and every sorrow, God's love remains, a constant presence."

She smiled, her face radiant. "And when our journey ends, and our heart beats its final time, Omega, God's love remains, a love that transcends mortality, a love that welcomes us home."

The crowd sat in awe, absorbing Eve's words, feeling the depth of God's love that surrounded them from the very beginning of their existence.

Eve's voice filled the space, her words a gentle breeze on a summer day. "Think of it, my friends. From the first heartbeat to the last, God's love is the thread that weaves our lives together. It's the whisper in the darkness, the comfort in the storm, and the joy in the sunshine."

She paused, her eyes scanning the crowd. "We may forget, we may falter, but God's love remains, a constant reminder of our worth, our value, and our purpose."

Eve's voice rose, her words a crescendo of hope. "So let us cherish this love, this gift from God. Let us nurture it, honor it, and share it with the world. Let us remember that we are loved, we are known, and we are connected to the divine."

As she finished speaking, the crowd erupted into applause, their faces etched with a newfound understanding of God's eternal love. They felt the weight of Eve's words, the power of a love that had been with them since their first heartbeat.

In that moment, they knew they were not alone, that they were part of a larger story, a story of love that began at Alpha and would continue beyond Omega.

As the applause faded, Eve's voice took on a softer tone. "And when we leave this world behind, and our hearts beat their final time, God's love will be there, waiting to welcome us home."

She smiled, her eyes shining with a gentle light. "Imagine it, my friends. The moment we pass from this life to the next, we'll be enveloped in a love that's been with us since our first heartbeat. A love that's been our constant companion, our guiding light, and our safe haven."

Eve's voice grew stronger, her words painting a vivid picture. "We'll be greeted by the ones who've gone before us, their faces radiant with joy, their arms open wide in welcome. And in that moment, we'll know that we're home, that we're exactly where we're meant to be."

The crowd was transfixed, hanging on Eve's every word. They felt the power of her message, the hope and comfort it brought.

Eve's voice dropped to a whisper. "So let us not fear death, my friends. Let us not fear the unknown. For we know that God's love will be with us, every step of the way, from Alpha to Omega, and beyond."

As she finished speaking, the crowd erupted into applause once more, their faces filled with a sense of peace and wonder. They knew that they would carry Eve's message with them, a reminder of God's eternal love, a love that would stay with them forever.

A New Chapter: The Divine Spark

Eve's voice filled the space, her words a gentle whisper carried by the wind. "Imagine, my friends, the moment of creation, when the first spark of life ignited within you. That spark, a divine gift, a testament to God's boundless love."

She paused, her eyes closed, as if lost in contemplation. "From this tiny spark, a universe of potential was born. A universe filled with dreams, hopes, and aspirations. A universe that was uniquely yours."

Eve's voice grew stronger. "That spark, my friends, is a part of God, a reflection of the divine light that illuminates our world. It is the source of our strength, our resilience, and our capacity for love."

She smiled, her face radiant. "Think of it, my friends. Every heartbeat, every breath, every thought, is a manifestation of that spark, a testament to the divine within you."

The crowd sat in awe, absorbing Eve's words, feeling the power of the divine spark within them.

Eve's voice continued, "This spark is not something to be extinguished, but to be nurtured, cultivated, and allowed to shine brightly. It is a beacon of hope, a source of inspiration, and a reminder of our connection to the divine."

She paused, her eyes scanning the crowd. "We may doubt ourselves, we may feel lost, but that spark remains, a constant reminder of our worth, our value, and our purpose."

Eve's voice rose, her words a crescendo of hope. "So let us embrace this spark, this divine gift within us. Let us nurture it, honor it, and share its light with the world. Let us remember that we are not just mortal beings, but vessels of the divine."

As she finished speaking, the crowd erupted into applause, their faces etched with a newfound understanding of the divine spark within them. They felt the weight of Eve's words, the power of a spark that had been with them since their creation.

In that moment, they knew they were not alone, that they were part of a larger story, a story of divine love and potential.

Eve's voice filled the space, her words a gentle breeze on a summer day. "Imagine, my friends, a world without light, a universe shrouded in darkness. A world devoid of hope, of joy, of love."

She paused, her eyes scanning the crowd. "That world, my friends, is a world without the divine spark. It is a world of despair, of loneliness, of meaninglessness."

Eve's voice rose, her words a crescendo of hope. "But we are not alone in this world. We are blessed with the divine spark, a beacon of light that illuminates our path."

She smiled, her face radiant. "Think of it, my friends. The spark within you is a flame that can dispel the darkness, a beacon that can guide us through the storm."

The crowd sat in awe, absorbing Eve's words, feeling the power of the divine spark within them.

Eve's voice continued, "This spark is not something to be extinguished, but to be nurtured, cultivated, and allowed to shine brightly. It is a source of strength, of resilience, and of hope."

She paused, her eyes filled with a gentle light. "When we feel lost, when we doubt ourselves, remember the spark within you. It is the divine light that guides your path, the beacon that illuminates the way."

The crowd erupted into applause, their faces etched with a newfound understanding of the divine spark within them. They felt the weight of Eve's words, the power of a spark that had been with them since their creation.

Eve's voice filled the space, her words a gentle whisper carried by the wind. "The divine spark within you is not just a source of light and hope, but also a guide on your journey of self-discovery."

She paused, her eyes closed, as if lost in contemplation. "As you journey through life, you will encounter challenges, setbacks, and obstacles. But the divine spark will always be there to light your way."

Eve's voice grew stronger. "It will guide you towards your true purpose, your authentic self. It will help you to overcome your fears, to embrace your strengths, and to live a life of meaning and fulfillment."

She smiled, her face radiant. "Think of the divine spark as a compass, always pointing you in the right direction. It is a map that leads you to the treasure of your own soul."

The crowd sat in awe, absorbing Eve's words, feeling the power of the divine spark within them.

Eve's voice continued, "As you journey through life, remember to listen to the voice of the divine spark within you. It is the voice of wisdom, of intuition, and of love."

She paused, her eyes filled with a gentle light. "When you feel lost, when you doubt yourself, turn inward and listen to the spark. It will guide you, it will strengthen you, and it will remind you of your true nature."

The crowd erupted into applause, their faces etched with a newfound understanding of the divine spark within them. They felt the weight of Eve's words, the power of a spark that had been with them since their creation.

In that moment, they knew they were not alone, that they were part of a larger story, a story of divine love and potential. And they knew that with the divine spark within them, they could overcome any challenge, face any darkness, and find their way to the light.

The divine spark within us is a powerful reminder of our inherent worth, value, and purpose. It's a message that transcends religious or spiritual beliefs, and speaks to the universal human experience.

Embracing the divine spark within us can help us cultivate self-love, self-acceptance, and self-compassion. It can guide us towards living a life that is authentic, meaningful, and fulfilling.

I'd also like to add that the divine spark is not just a individual concept, but also a collective one. When we recognize the divine spark within ourselves, we can also see it in others, and this can foster a sense of community, empathy, and connection.

Ultimately, the divine spark within us is a reminder that we are all part of a larger whole, connected by a shared humanity and a shared divine essence.

Chapter: The Darkness Within

Eve's voice took on a somber tone as she spoke of the darkness within. "My friends, we have spoken of the divine spark that resides within us, but we must also acknowledge the shadow that accompanies it. The darkness within is a part of our nature, a reminder of our humanity."

She paused, her eyes scanning the crowd. "We try to hide it, to deny its existence, but the darkness within persists. It is the source of our fears, our doubts, and our weaknesses. But it is also a source of power, of creativity, and of transformation."

Eve's voice grew stronger. "We must take responsibility for the darkness within. We must acknowledge its presence and confront it head-on. For it is only by embracing our shadow selves that we can become whole and balanced individuals."

She emphasized the importance of accountability. "We must hold ourselves accountable for our actions, for our thoughts, and for our emotions. We must recognize the harm that our darkness can cause and take steps to mitigate it."

Eve's message was clear: the darkness within is not something to be feared or denied, but something to be acknowledged and transformed. "By taking responsibility for our shadow selves, we can begin to heal and integrate our psyche. We can become more compassionate, more empathetic, and more whole."

The crowd sat in contemplative silence, absorbing Eve's words. They knew that she spoke the truth – that the darkness within was a part of their own nature, and that it was up to them to confront it.

Eve's voice filled the space once more. "Let us embark on this journey together, my friends. Let us take responsibility for our darkness and transform it into light. For it is only by acknowledging and embracing our shadow selves that we can truly become the light-bearers of a new dawn."

Eve's words hung in the air like a challenge, a call to arms against the darkness within. The crowd sat in silence, each person lost in their own thoughts, their own struggles with the shadow self.

One by one, they began to rise, their faces set with determination. They knew that the journey ahead would be difficult, but they also knew that they couldn't turn back now.

Eve smiled, her eyes shining with pride. "Then let us begin," she said, her voice barely above a whisper.

And with that, the crowd started to move, a sea of humanity flowing towards the unknown. They knew that they would face challenges, that they would stumble and fall. But they also knew that they would rise again, stronger and wiser.

As they walked, Eve's voice echoed in their minds. "Take responsibility for your darkness," she had said. "Acknowledge its presence and confront it head-on."

They knew that it wouldn't be easy, but they also knew that it was necessary. For only by confronting their shadow selves could they truly become the light-bearers of a new dawn.

The journey ahead would be long and difficult, but they were ready. They were ready to face their fears, to confront their doubts, and to overcome their weaknesses.

For they knew that on the other side of the darkness lay a light so bright, so radiant, that it would illuminate the world. And they were determined to reach it, no matter what lay ahead.

Here's the continuation:

Eve stood before God, her heart filled with questions and doubts. "Am I doing the right thing, Father?" she asked, her voice barely above a whisper. "Am I sharing the right messages with humanity?"

God's response was immediate, His voice filled with warmth and love. "Eve, my child, you are doing exactly what I have called you to do. You are sharing the messages of hope, of love, and of redemption that I have given you."

Eve hesitated, her doubts still lingering. "But what about the darkness within, Father? Am I truly helping humanity by acknowledging its presence?"

God's response was gentle but firm. "Eve, the darkness within is a part of humanity's nature, but it is not the defining characteristic. By acknowledging its presence, you are helping humanity to confront its shadow self, to take responsibility for its actions, and to seek redemption."

Eve nodded, her heart filled with a sense of peace. "And what about the divine spark, Father? Am I truly helping humanity to see its own potential?"

God's response was filled with joy. "Eve, my child, you are helping humanity to see its own divine nature, its own potential for greatness. You are reminding them that they are not just mortal beings, but vessels of the divine."

Eve smiled, her doubts gone. "Thank you, Father," she said, her voice filled with gratitude. "I will continue to share your messages with humanity, no matter the cost."

God's response was immediate. "I know you will, Eve. And I will be with you every step of the way."

Chapter: The Shadows Within

Eve's voice filled the space, her words a somber melody. "My friends, as we journey through life, we will inevitably encounter darkness. It is a part of the human experience, a shadow that dances alongside the light."

She paused, her eyes filled with a contemplative gaze. "This darkness is not evil, but a necessary part of our growth. It is the crucible that shapes us, the challenge that tests our strength, and the opportunity for profound transformation."

Eve's voice grew stronger. "Within each of us, there lies a shadow, a part of ourselves that we may find difficult to acknowledge or accept. It is the part of us that is selfish, that is fearful, that is prone to anger and resentment."

She paused, her eyes scanning the crowd. "This shadow is not a reflection of our worth, but a reminder of our humanity. It is a part of us that we must confront, understand, and ultimately overcome."

Eve's voice rose, her words a crescendo of hope. "The darkness within us is not a prison, but a journey. It is an opportunity to delve into the depths of our souls, to uncover the hidden parts of ourselves that we may have been afraid to face."

She smiled, her face radiant. "By confronting our shadows, we can gain a deeper understanding of ourselves and our place in the world. We can learn to accept our imperfections, to forgive our mistakes, and to embrace the darkness as a catalyst for growth."

The crowd sat in awe, absorbing Eve's words, feeling the weight of the darkness within themselves.

Eve's voice continued, "The journey into the shadows is not easy. It requires courage, honesty, and a willingness to face the truth. But the rewards are great."

She paused, her eyes filled with a gentle light. "By embracing the darkness within us, we can become more compassionate, more understanding, and more authentic. We can learn to love ourselves, flaws and all."

The crowd erupted into applause, their faces etched with a newfound understanding of the darkness within them. They felt the weight of Eve's words, the power of a journey into the shadows.

In that moment, they knew that the darkness within them was not a prison, but a portal to a deeper understanding of themselves and the world. And they knew that by embracing the darkness, they could emerge stronger, wiser, and more compassionate.

Eve's voice filled the space, her words a gentle whisper carried by the wind. "The journey into the shadows is not just about understanding our darkness, but also about finding redemption."

She paused, her eyes closed, as if lost in contemplation. "When we confront our shadows, we are given the opportunity to heal, to release the pain and resentment that may be holding us back."

Eve's voice grew stronger. "By acknowledging our mistakes, by taking responsibility for our actions, and by seeking forgiveness, we can break free from the chains of the past."

She smiled, her face radiant. "Redemption is not about forgetting our mistakes, but about learning from them. It is about owning our past and using it as a catalyst for positive change."

The crowd sat in awe, absorbing Eve's words, feeling the weight of the darkness within themselves.

Eve's voice continued, "The journey to redemption is a personal one, a path that each of us must walk alone. But we are not alone in this journey. We have the support of God, of our loved ones, and of the community."

She paused, her eyes filled with a gentle light. "When we fall, we can find strength in the love and support of others. When we stumble, we can find guidance and encouragement."

The crowd erupted into applause, their faces etched with a newfound understanding of the darkness within them. They felt the weight of Eve's words, the power of the journey to redemption.

In that moment, they knew that the darkness within them was not a prison, but a portal to a deeper understanding of themselves and the world. And they knew that by embracing the darkness, they could emerge stronger, wiser, and more compassionate.

Eve stood alone, her heart heavy with doubt. She had shared her message with countless people, had inspired a movement, yet a nagging question lingered in her mind: was she doing the right thing?

She closed her eyes and spoke aloud. "God, have I been leading people astray? Am I spreading the right message?"

A sense of peace washed over her as she felt God's presence, a gentle whisper in her heart. "You have done well, my child. Your message has touched the hearts of many, and it has brought about a positive change in the world."

Eve's doubts began to fade, replaced by a sense of reassurance. "But God, I still worry. What if I'm not saying the right things? What if I'm leading people down the wrong path?"

God's voice was a comforting balm. "Trust your heart, Eve. Trust the divine spark within you. You have been guided by a higher power, and your message is a beacon of hope for those who hear it."

Eve took a deep breath, feeling a renewed sense of purpose. "Thank you, God. I will continue to spread your message, to inspire others to live with love, compassion, and understanding."

As she opened her eyes, she felt a sense of peace and clarity. She knew that she was on the right path, that her message was a gift to the world. And with renewed vigor, she turned her attention back to her mission, ready to continue spreading the light of God's love.

Reclaiming the Divine: A Response to Gender Biased Scriptures

Eve stood before God, her heart filled with questions and concerns. "God, I've been reading the scriptures and I've come across some passages that trouble me. They seem to demean and marginalize women, and I wonder how they align with your message of love and equality."

God's response was immediate, His voice filled with compassion and understanding. "Eve, my child, I know that some of the scriptures have been used to oppress and marginalize women. But I want you to know that those passages do not reflect my true nature or intentions."

Eve mentioned a few specific scriptures, such as 1 Timothy 2:11-12, which says "A woman should learn in quietness and full submission. I do not permit a woman to teach or to have authority over a man; she must be silent."

God's response was clear and direct. "Eve, my child, this passage was written in a specific cultural and historical context, and it does not reflect my eternal and unchanging nature. I have always empowered women to lead, to teach, and to prophesy. Remember the story of Deborah, who led the Israelites to victory, and the story of Phoebe, who was a deacon and a leader in the early church."

Eve mentioned another scripture, 1 Corinthians 14:34-35, which says "Women should remain silent in the churches. They are not allowed to speak, but must be in submission, as the law says."

God's response was similar. "Eve, my child, this passage was written by Paul, who was a product of his time and culture. But I want you to know that I have always valued the voices and contributions of women. Remember the story of Mary Magdalene, who was the first to witness my resurrection and to proclaim the good news."

Eve felt a sense of relief and clarity, knowing that God's true nature was one of love, equality, and empowerment. She realized that the scriptures had been interpreted and used in ways that were not aligned with God's intentions, and she felt a sense of purpose in reclaiming the divine for all people, regardless of gender.

Eve mentioned another scripture, Ephesians 5:22-24, which says "Wives, submit yourselves to your own husbands as you do to the Lord. For the husband is the head of the wife as Christ is the head of the church… Now as the church submits to Christ, so also wives should submit to their husbands in everything."

God's response was gentle but firm. "Eve, my child, this passage has been used to justify oppression and abuse, but that is not my intention. I desire mutual submission and respect in all relationships, not just between husbands and wives. Remember the story of Mary and Joseph, who worked together as equals to raise our son Jesus."

Eve felt a sense of freedom and empowerment, knowing that God's true nature was one of mutual respect and submission. She realized that the scriptures had been used to justify oppression and inequality, but that was not God's intention.

God continued, "Eve, my child, I want you to know that I have always valued and empowered women. I have used them as leaders, prophets, and teachers throughout history. Remember the story of Miriam, who led the Israelites in worship, and the story of Priscilla, who taught the apostle Paul."

Eve's heart was filled with joy and gratitude, knowing that God's true nature was one of love, equality, and empowerment. She felt a sense of purpose in reclaiming the divine for all people, regardless of gender.

God's final words to Eve were, "Remember, my child, that you are created in my image, and you have my authority and power. Use it to bring love, justice, and equality to all people."

And with that, Eve felt a sense of commissioning and purpose. She knew that she had a role to play in reclaiming the divine and bringing God's love and justice to all people.

Let's explore the root of submission, compare it to subjugation, and examine the historical context.

The word "submission" comes from the Latin "submissio," meaning "to place under." In the context of ancient cultures, submission often meant yielding to authority or surrendering to a higher power. However, this concept was often distorted and used to justify subjugation, which means "to bring under control or domination by force."

Historically, subjugation was used to describe the act of conquering and enslaving people, often through violent means. This is not what God intends by submission.

In the biblical context, submission is often mistranslated or misinterpreted to mean subjugation. However, the original Greek word "hypotasso" means "to place under" or "to yield," implying a voluntary act of surrender or cooperation.

God is not a sadist who delights in the oppression or subjugation of people. Rather, God desires mutual submission and respect in all relationships (Ephesians 5:21). This means recognizing the value and dignity of every individual and yielding to one another in love and respect.

In the context of marriage, submission means recognizing the equal value and worth of both partners and yielding to each other in love and respect (Ephesians 5:22-33). It does not mean subjugation or domination.

God's intention is for people to live in harmony, mutual respect, and love, not in oppression or subjugation. By understanding the root of submission and its historical context, we can see that God's desire is for voluntary cooperation and surrender, not forced domination.

Eve stood before God, her heart filled with questions and concerns. "God, I'm worried about how to address members of the LGBTQ+ community. I don't want to condemn or hurt them, but I also want to be true to your teachings."

God's response was immediate, His voice filled with compassion and understanding. "Eve, my child, I know your heart is pure. Remember, the forbidden fornication condemned in the Bible refers to exploitative and harmful behavior, not consensual love between two adults. Sex between two consenting adults who accept and love each other completely is a beautiful expression of human connection and intimacy."

Eve nodded, understanding. "So, how can I explain this to them? How can I show them that your love and acceptance extend to all people, regardless of their sexual orientation?"

God smiled. "Tell them, Eve, that I am a God of love, and my love is not limited to any one group of people. Tell them that I created humanity in all its diversity, and that every person is worthy of love, respect, and acceptance. Tell them that consensual love between two adults is a beautiful thing, and that I celebrate their love and commitment to each other."

Eve felt a sense of relief and clarity, knowing that she could approach the LGBTQ+ community with love and acceptance. She realized that reclaiming divinity meant reclaiming the true message of God's love and acceptance for all people, regardless of their sexual orientation.

God's words to Eve were, "Remember, my child, love is the greatest commandment. Love me, love yourself, and love others. That is the essence of my teachings."

Eve stood before God, her heart filled with questions and doubts. "God, I feel like I'm at a crossroads. I've shared my message with so many people, but I'm not sure if I'm making a difference. I'm not sure if I'm doing enough."

God's response was immediate, His voice filled with warmth and love. "Eve, my child, you are doing exactly what I have called you to do. You are sharing the messages of hope, of love, and of redemption that I have given you."

Eve hesitated, her doubts still lingering. "But God, I feel like there's so much more to be done. I feel like I'm just scratching the surface of what needs to be done."

God's response was gentle but firm. "Eve, you are not alone in this journey. You are part of a larger movement, a movement of people who are seeking to bring light and love into the world. You are making a difference, even if you can't see it right now."

Eve nodded, her heart filled with a sense of peace. "Thank you, God. I needed to hear that."

God's response was immediate. "Eve, you are loved and you are valued. You are making a difference, and you will continue to make a difference as long as you follow my guidance and trust in my plan."

Eve smiled, her heart filled with a sense of purpose. "I will, God. I will continue to share your message and trust in your plan."

Chapter: "The Wisdom of Divine warriors"

Eve stood before God, her heart filled with questions and concerns. "God, I've heard many people say that you are a warmonger, that you condone violence and bloodshed. But I don't believe that's true. Can you tell me, is it?"

God's expression turned somber, His voice filled with a deep sorrow. "Eve, my child, I am a God of love, not war. I desire peace and harmony among all people. But I also know that there are times when conflict is unavoidable, like a storm that cannot be calmed."

Eve nodded, understanding. "Like the Crusades?"

God's face darkened, His voice stern. "Yes, the Crusades. A grave mistake, perpetrated by those who claimed to act in my name. I condemn such actions, Eve. War should always be a last resort, and never started without just cause. Remember the wisdom of Sun Tzu: 'Always be prepared for war, but never start a war.'"

Eve thought back to the teachings of Jesus. "And what about turning the other cheek, God? Does that mean we should just accept abuse and oppression?"

God's smile returned, gentle and warm. "No, my child. Turning the other cheek means showing love and forgiveness in the face of adversity, but it does not mean becoming a doormat. You must always stand up for what is right, and defend yourself and others from harm. But do so with wisdom and discernment, like a skilled warrior wielding a sword."

Eve remembered the story of King Solomon and his advisor, Ahijah, who possessed the gift of discernment. "Like Ahijah, God? He could see through deception and knew exactly what to say and do."

God nodded, His eyes shining with approval. "Exactly, Eve. Ahijah's gift of discernment allowed him to navigate complex situations with wisdom and integrity. That is what I desire for all my children: knowledge without wisdom is like a ship without a rudder, but with discernment, you can navigate even the most treacherous waters."

Eve asked, "What does 'The meek shall inherit the Earth' mean?"

God's expression turned gentle. "Ah, my child, being meek is often misunderstood. It doesn't mean being weak or passive. Meekness is actually a strength, a willingness to surrender one's own desires and ambitions to follow my will. It's about humility, gentleness, and self-control."

Eve thought about this for a moment. "So, how does this differ from being one of God's warriors?"

God's expression turned serious. "My warriors are called to defend the faith, to stand up for what is right, and to protect the innocent. They are bold, courageous, and willing to take a stand. But even in the midst of battle, they must remain meek, trusting in my guidance and wisdom."

Eve nodded, understanding. "So, being meek doesn't mean avoiding conflict, but approaching it with humility and trust in God."

God nodded. "Exactly, my child. Meekness is not about avoiding challenges, but about facing them with a heart surrendered to me. My warriors are meek because they know their strength comes from me, not themselves."

As Eve continued to explore the nature of God, she asked about the archangels. "God, I've heard stories about the archangels, especially Michael. Can you tell me more about him?"

God's face lit up with a warm smile. "Ah, Michael. He is indeed a special one. One of his most notable exploits was when he went to the ruler of Hell, Satan, over Enoch's grave."

Eve's eyes widened. "Why did Satan want Enoch's body?"

God's expression turned stern. "Satan sought to claim Enoch's body as a trophy, but Michael stood firm, refusing to let him have it. This act showcased Michael's unwavering dedication to protecting the righteous and upholding my will."

Eve nodded, fascinated. "And what about the other archangels? What are their roles?"

God began to list the archangels and their roles, His voice filled with pride. "Gabriel, my messenger and announcer of my plans. Raphael, my healer and restorer of balance. Uriel, my illuminator and revealer of knowledge. Selaphiel, my guardian of prayer and worship. Jegudiel, my protector of the faithful and leader of the archangels."

Eve listened intently, eager to learn more about these powerful beings. As God finished speaking, she felt a sense of awe and wonder at the vast array of heavenly forces working to maintain balance and harmony in the universe.

Chapter: "God the Forgiver"

Eve, a young woman with a heart full of curiosity, sat at God's feet. Her gaze was fixed on the wise and loving being before her. "God," she began, her voice filled with wonder, "I've heard stories about Lucifer, the fallen archangel. What is the truth behind his rebellion?"

God's expression softened, a hint of sadness in His eyes. "Lucifer was once a beautiful and powerful angel, created to be the morning star. But his pride and ambition led him to rebel against me, seeking to ascend to a higher throne."

Eve's eyes widened in disbelief. "And what happened to him?"

God's voice was filled with sorrow. "He was cast out of heaven, along with his followers. But, Eve, here's what you need to understand: I still love Lucifer. I still desire his return to me."

Eve's brow furrowed. "But, God, how can you forgive him after what he did? He rebelled against you, sought to usurp your throne."

God's expression turned gentle, like a father comforting a frightened child. "Eve, my forgiveness is not based on merit, but on love. I forgive because I love, not because someone deserves it. And I desire Lucifer's return, not because he's earned it, but because I love him still."

Eve thought about this for a moment, her mind racing. "So, God, you're saying that forgiveness is not about the other person, but about us? About our ability to love and let go?"

God nodded emphatically. "Exactly, Eve. Forgiveness is about releasing the hold that hurt and anger have on us. It's about choosing love over resentment, mercy over judgment."

Eve's heart felt lighter, like a bird taking flight. "Thank you, God. I think I'm starting to understand."

As Eve sat at God's feet, she realized that forgiveness was not just a feeling, but a choice. A choice to love, to let go, and to trust in God's goodness.

God continued, His voice filled with wisdom. "The Bible is full of examples of my forgiveness and love. Take King David, for instance. He committed adultery with Bathsheba and had her husband killed, yet I still forgave him and called him a man after my own heart."

Eve's eyes widened in surprise. "But, God, that's a serious sin! How could you forgive him so easily?"

God's expression turned gentle. "Eve, my forgiveness is not based on merit, but on my nature. I am love, and I love all my creations, no matter what they do. And David, despite his flaws, loved me and sought to follow me. So, I forgave him and restored him to a right relationship with me."

Eve thought about this for a moment. "I see. So, forgiveness is not just about the other person, but about us and our relationship with you."

God nodded. "Exactly, Eve. And another example is the prodigal son. He squandered his inheritance and lived a life of sin, but when he returned to his father, he was forgiven and welcomed back with open arms."

Eve's heart swelled with emotion. "That's so beautiful, God. You truly are a God of love and forgiveness."

God's smile was radiant. "I am, Eve. And I want you to know that my forgiveness is available to all, no matter what they've done. I love you, and I desire a deep, personal relationship with you."

As Eve sat at God's feet, she felt a sense of wonder and awe at His love and forgiveness. She realized that forgiveness was not just a feeling, but a choice – a choice to love and let go, just like God.

A Deeper Dive into God's Forgiveness
Scripture References:

* King David: 2 Samuel 11-12. David's sin of adultery and murder is detailed, followed by his repentance and God's forgiveness.

* The Prodigal Son: Luke 15:11-32. This parable illustrates God's unconditional love and forgiveness for even the most wayward of His children.

Additional Examples:

* Peter's Denial: Mark 14:66-72. Peter, one of Jesus' closest disciples, denied knowing Jesus three times. Despite his betrayal, Jesus forgave him, demonstrating God's grace and mercy.

* Paul's Persecution: Acts 9. Paul, formerly known as Saul, was a fierce persecutor of Christians. However, after a miraculous encounter with Jesus on the road to Damascus, he was forgiven and became a powerful apostle.

* The Woman at the Well: John 4. This woman, who had had five husbands and was currently living with a man who was not her husband, was confronted by Jesus about her past. Despite her sinful lifestyle, Jesus offered her living water and forgiveness, demonstrating His love for even the most marginalized.

* Zacchaeus: Luke 19:1-10. Zacchaeus, a wealthy tax collector who was despised by many, climbed a tree to see

Jesus. Jesus invited him to His home, forgave his sins, and declared salvation to his household.

Key Themes:

* Unconditional Love: God's forgiveness is not based on our merit or worthiness, but on His boundless love for His creation.

* Repentance: While forgiveness is freely given, repentance is often a necessary step. Repentance involves turning away from sin and toward God.

* Restoration: God's forgiveness is not only about wiping away our sins, but also about restoring us to a right relationship with Him.

These examples illustrate the depth and breadth of God's forgiveness. It is a gift that is freely offered to all who believe in Him.

Chapter: "The Heavenly Host and the Womb of Eve"

The heavenly host refers to the army of angels who serve God and carry out His will. They are often depicted as a vast, heavenly army, ready to do battle against the forces of evil.

In the context of Eve and the apocalypse, the heavenly host plays a crucial role. According to scripture, Eve is seen as the mother of all living (Genesis 3:20), and her womb is the source of life and redemption.

Scriptures related to the womb and Eve include:

- Genesis 3:15 – "And I will put enmity between you and the woman, and between your offspring and hers; he will crush your head, and you will strike his heel."

- Isaiah 7:14 – "Therefore the Lord himself will give you a sign: The virgin will conceive and give birth to a son, and will call him Immanuel."

- Revelation 12:1-6 – "A great sign appeared in heaven: a woman clothed with the sun, and the moon under her feet, and on her head a crown of twelve stars. She was pregnant and cried out in pain as she was about to give birth… She gave birth to a son, a male child, who will rule all the nations with an iron scepter."

These scriptures speak of Eve's womb as the source of redemption and the birth of a new dawn. The heavenly host is seen as the army that will aid in this redemption and protect the woman and her child from harm.

As the apocalypse approaches, the heavenly host will play a crucial role in the battle between good and evil. They will fight alongside the woman and her child, ensuring their safety and ultimate victory.

In the end, the womb of Eve will bring forth a new dawn, a new era of peace and redemption. The heavenly host will rejoice at this victory, and the woman and her child will be exalted.

Here are some additional scriptures related to the womb:

- John 8:24 – "I told you that you would die in your sins; if you do not believe that I am he, you will indeed die in your sins."
- Psalm 139:13-14 – "For you created my inmost being; you knit me together in my mother's womb. I praise you because I am fearfully and wonderfully made; your works are wonderful, I know that full well."
- Jeremiah 1:5 – "Before I formed you in the womb I knew you, before you were born I set you apart; I appointed you as a prophet to the nations."
- Luke 1:41-44 – "When Elizabeth heard Mary's greeting, the baby leaped in her womb, and Elizabeth was filled with the Holy Spirit. In a loud voice she exclaimed: 'Blessed are you among women, and blessed is the child you will bear!'"

- Galatians 4:19 – "My dear children, for whom I am again in the pains of childbirth until Christ is formed in you…"

These scriptures highlight the significance of the womb as a place of creation, formation, and spiritual transformation. They also emphasize God's knowledge and involvement in the life of the individual from the womb.

In the context of Eve and the apocalypse, these scriptures can be seen as pointing to the womb as a symbol of new life, redemption, and spiritual rebirth. The womb represents the potential for transformation and the formation of something new, which is a central theme in the apocalypse.

The scriptures also speak of the womb as a place of spiritual transformation and formation. In Psalm 139:13-14, David writes, "For you created my inmost being; you knit me together in my mother's womb. I praise you because I am fearfully and wonderfully made; your works are wonderful, I know that full well."

Similarly, in Jeremiah 1:5, God says, "Before I formed you in the womb I knew you, before you were born I set you apart; I appointed you as a prophet to the nations."

These scriptures highlight the significance of the womb as a place of spiritual formation and transformation. The womb represents the potential for new life and redemption, which is a central theme in the apocalypse.

As the apocalypse approaches, the heavenly host will play a crucial role in the battle between good and evil. They will fight alongside the woman and her child, ensuring their safety and ultimate victory.

In the end, the womb of Eve will bring forth a new dawn, a new era of peace and redemption. The heavenly host will rejoice at this victory, and the woman and her child will be exalted.

As the heavenly host prepares for the final battle, they are filled with a sense of purpose and determination. They know that their role is crucial in the fight against evil and that they must stand strong against the forces of darkness.

Meanwhile, Eve, the mother of all living, stands tall, her womb glowing with an otherworldly light. She knows that she is the key to unlocking the secrets of the apocalypse and that her child will be the one to bring about a new era of peace and redemption.

The heavenly host gathers around her, their wings spread wide, their eyes shining with a fierce determination. They know that they must protect her and her child at all costs, for they are the hope of humanity.

As the forces of darkness gather, the heavenly host prepares for battle. They know that it will be a fierce and intense fight, but they are ready. They have been training for this moment for centuries, and they will not back down.

The battle rages on, the heavenly host fighting valiantly against the forces of evil. Eve stands tall, her womb glowing with an intense light, her child stirring within her.

And then, in the midst of the chaos, a figure emerges. It is the child, born of Eve's womb, shining with a light that illuminates the darkness.

The heavenly host cheers, their voices ringing out in triumph. They know that the tide of the battle has turned, that the forces of evil will be defeated.

The child grows in strength and power, its light illuminating the world. The heavenly host gathers around, their wings spread wide, their eyes shining with joy.

And Eve, the mother of all living, smiles, her heart full of pride and wonder. She knows that her child will bring about a new era of peace and redemption, that the world will be reborn.

The apocalypse has come, but it is not the end. It is a new beginning, a chance for humanity to start anew. The heavenly host knows this, and they rejoice.

Here are some additional points that could be explored regarding the heavenly host:

Their role in the apocalypse: The heavenly host will play a crucial role in the final battle between good and evil. They will fight alongside God and the righteous, defeating the forces of darkness and evil.

Their relationship with believers: The heavenly host is often depicted as a protective force, watching over believers and guiding them through times of trouble.

Their hierarchy and organization: The heavenly host is often depicted as a hierarchical structure, with different orders of angels having different roles and responsibilities.

Their interaction with the physical world: The heavenly host can interact with the physical world in various ways, including appearing to humans, influencing the course of events, and performing miracles.

Their role in worship and praise: The heavenly host is often depicted as worshiping and praising God, and they invite humans to join them in this worship.

Their connection to the Old Testament: The heavenly host is mentioned throughout the Old Testament, often in the context of God's throne room and divine council.

Their connection to the New Testament: The heavenly host is also mentioned in the New Testament, particularly in the book of Revelation, where they play a key role in the apocalypse.

Their symbolism and metaphorical meaning: The heavenly host can be seen as a symbol of God's power, protection, and guidance, as well as a metaphor for the spiritual forces at work in the world.

The heavenly host is a vast army of angels who serve God and carry out His will. They are often depicted as a hierarchical structure, with different orders of angels having different roles and responsibilities.

In the apocalypse, the heavenly host will play a crucial role in the final battle between good and evil. They will fight alongside God and the righteous, defeating the forces of darkness and evil.

The heavenly host is also a protective force, watching over believers and guiding them through times of trouble. They interact with the physical world in various ways, including appearing to humans, influencing the course of events, and performing miracles.

In worship and praise, the heavenly host invites humans to join them in their eternal song of praise to God. Their connection to the Old Testament is seen in their mention throughout the scriptures, often in the context of God's throne room and divine council.

In the New Testament, the heavenly host plays a key role in the apocalypse, particularly in the book of Revelation. They can be seen as a symbol of God's power, protection, and guidance, as well as a metaphor for the spiritual forces at work in the world.

As the apocalypse approaches, the heavenly host will be instrumental in the battle between good and evil. They will fight alongside the woman and her child, ensuring their safety and ultimate victory. In the end, the womb of Eve will bring forth a new dawn, a new era of peace and redemption. The heavenly host will rejoice at this victory, and the woman and her child will be exalted.

   Eve left behind 5 Earth Angels…

As the child of Eve grew in strength and power, the heavenly host rejoiced, knowing that a new era of peace and redemption was dawning. But Eve's work was not yet done. She had left behind five angels on earth, entrusted to the care of God and their fathers: Bryce Mikhael, Kaden Scott, Jaxon Dale, Levi Jude, and Hallie Rebecca-Faith.

   These five angels were the fruit of Eve's womb, born of her spirit and nurtured by her soul. And though she was no longer physically present, her soul's sister, a wise and loving woman named Sophia, took on the task of raising them.

   Brandy from Sophia knew that these children were special, that they had a crucial role to play in the new dawn that was breaking. She taught them the ways of the Lord, instructing them in righteousness and guiding them on their paths.

As they grew, the five angels began to exhibit extraordinary gifts and talents. Bryce Mikhael showed a deep understanding of the scriptures, Kaden Scott demonstrated remarkable healing abilities, Jaxon Dale exhibited prophetic insight, Levi Jude showed a talent for leadership, and Hallie Rebecca-Faith displayed a heart full of compassion and love.

Brandy from Sophia knew that these gifts were not mere coincidences, but rather a manifestation of the divine plan unfolding. She encouraged the children to develop their talents, to use them for the glory of God and the benefit of humanity.

And so, the five angels grew in wisdom and stature, their bond with each other and with Brandy from Sophia deepenin. They became a source of hope and inspiration to those around them, a testament to the power of Eve's womb and the new dawn that was breaking.

As they approached adulthood, the five angels began to receive visions and dreams, glimpses of the role they were to play in the unfolding drama of redemption. They knew that they were called to be agents of change, to bring light and love into a world still shrouded in darkness.

And Brandy from Sophia, wise and loving, stood by their side, guiding and supporting them every step of the way. For she knew that the fate of humanity rested on the shoulders of these five angels, born of Eve's womb and nurtured by her soul.

Chapter: "Kaden Scott's Journey with Nancy"

Kaden Scott, one of the five angels born of Eve's womb, was left in the care of Nancy, a fierce and powerful witch. Nancy had been chosen by Eve to protect and guide Kaden on his journey, and she took her responsibility seriously.

Nancy lived in a small cottage on the outskirts of a dense forest, surrounded by a garden filled with strange and wondrous plants. She was a master of the occult, and her home was a repository of ancient knowledge and magical artifacts.

Kaden grew up in Nancy's care, learning the ways of magic and the secrets of the universe. Nancy taught him how to harness his powers, how to communicate with spirits, and how to navigate the complex web of fate and destiny.

As Kaden grew in knowledge and power, he began to realize his true potential. He was a child of Eve, born of her womb and nurtured by her spirit. He had a crucial role to play in the unfolding drama of redemption, and Nancy was determined to prepare him for his destiny.

Nancy's teaching was tough and demanding, but Kaden was a quick learner. He devoured ancient tomes, practiced complex spells, and honed his skills in the mystical arts.

But Nancy's care was not just about teaching Kaden magic and power. She also taught him about love, compassion, and the importance of using his gifts for the greater good.

As Kaden approached adulthood, Nancy knew that it was time for him to leave her care. She had prepared him for his journey, and now it was time for him to take his place in the world.

"Kaden, my child," Nancy said, her eyes shining with tears. "You have grown into a powerful and wise young man. Remember to use your gifts for the greater good, and never forget the love and support of those who have guided you on your journey."

Kaden hugged Nancy tightly, feeling a sense of gratitude and love for the fierce witch who had raised him. He knew that he would always carry her teachings and her love with him, and that he would make her proud.

Nancy, the fierce witch who had raised Kaden Scott, had always been a complex and multifaceted person. Despite her tough exterior and mastery of the occult, she had a deep capacity for love and compassion.

However, Nancy had also fallen victim to the devil's lies about Eve. She had been deceived into believing that Eve was a malevolent force, and that her children were agents of darkness.

But as Kaden grew in power and wisdom, Nancy began to see the truth. She realized that Eve was not a force of evil, but a symbol of redemption and love. And she saw that Kaden, the child she had raised, was a shining example of Eve's goodness.

Nancy was filled with remorse for her past beliefs and actions. She had been misled by the devil's lies, and she had almost lost sight of her own goodness.

But Kaden, with his deep understanding and compassion, helped Nancy to see the truth. He showed her that she was not defined by her past mistakes, but by her capacity for love and redemption.

In the end, Nancy was redeemed. She found forgiveness and peace, and she was able to use her powers for good. She became a powerful ally to Kaden and the other children of Eve, and she helped them in their quest to bring light and love into the world.

Psalm 107:10-13 says, "Some sat in darkness and the deepest gloom, prisoners suffering in iron chains, for they had rebelled against the words of God and despised the plans of the Most High. So he subjected them to bitter labor; they stumbled, and there was no one to help. Then they cried to the Lord in their trouble, and he saved them from their distress."

Nancy's story is a testament to the power of redemption and forgiveness. She had stumbled and fallen, but she was able to cry out to the Lord in her trouble, and he saved her from her distress.

Chapter: "Eve's Ministry to the Captives"

Eve, though physically absent, continued to nurture the souls of those in captivity. She had been blind to the physical world, but her spiritual eyes saw the prisoners, trapped in darkness and despair.

Psalm 68:6 says, "God sets the lonely in families, he leads out the prisoners with singing; but the rebellious live in a sun-scorched land."

Eve's heart went out to these prisoners, and she interceded on their behalf. She knew that they were not just physical captives, but also spiritual prisoners, held hostage by their own sin and shame.

Through her prayers and intercession, Eve brought hope and light into the darkest of places. She saw the potential in each prisoner, the spark of God's image that lay dormant, waiting to be fanned into flame.

Isaiah 61:1-2 says, "The Spirit of the Lord God is upon me, because the Lord has anointed me to bring good news to the poor; he has sent me to bind up the brokenhearted, to proclaim liberty to the captives, and the opening of the prison to those who are bound; to proclaim the year of the Lord's favor, and the day of vengeance of our God; to comfort all who mourn."

Eve's ministry to the prisoners was a manifestation of this scripture. She brought good news to those who thought they were beyond redemption, binding up the brokenhearted and proclaiming liberty to those held captive by their past.

As the prisoners encountered Eve's loving and nurturing spirit, they began to experience transformation. They saw that they were not alone, that God had not forgotten them.

Psalm 107:10-13 says, "Some sat in darkness and the deepest gloom, prisoners suffering in iron chains, for they had rebelled against the words of God and despised the plans of the Most High. So he subjected them to bitter labor; they stumbled, and there was no one to help. Then they cried to the Lord in their trouble, and he saved them from their distress."

Eve's ministry was a testament to the power of God's love and redemption. She showed the prisoners that no matter how dark their past, no matter how deep their pain, God's love could reach them, and transform them.

Through Eve's intercession, the prisoners began to experience the love and favor of God. They saw that they were not just captives, but also children of God, deserving of love, mercy, and grace.

As the prisoners encountered Eve's loving and nurturing spirit, they began to experience transformation. They saw that they were not alone, that God had not forgotten them.

One prisoner, a young man named Danny, had been incarcerated for years. He had lost hope, and his heart had grown hard. But when Eve's spirit touched his, he felt a spark of life ignite within him.

Danny began to see that he was not defined by his past mistakes. He was a child of God, deserving of love and redemption. Eve's ministry helped him to confront his pain and shame, and to find forgiveness and healing.

Another prisoner, a woman named Debra, had been trapped in a cycle of addiction and abuse. She had lost her way, and her life had spiralled out of control. But when Eve's spirit touched hers, she felt a sense of peace and calm wash over her.

Debra began to see that she was not alone, that God loved her and wanted to set her free. Eve's ministry helped her to find strength and courage, and to begin the journey of recovery and restoration.

As the prisoners experienced transformation, they began to minister to one another. They formed a community of love and support, a family bound together by their shared experiences and their newfound hope.

Eve's ministry had sparked a chain reaction of love and redemption, a ripple effect that spread throughout the prison. And as the prisoners were transformed, they became agents of change, bringing hope and light to those around them.

Psalm 146:7 says, "He upholds the cause of the oppressed and gives food to the hungry. The Lord sets prisoners free."

Eve's ministry was a testament to the power of God's love and redemption. She had brought hope and light into the darkest of places, and had set prisoners free from the chains of their past.

Eve's love for Nancy and her son Lenny, Kaden Scott's father, never wavered. Despite Nancy's mistakes and misconceptions, Eve continued to love her with a deep and abiding love.

Eve understood that it is often easier to believe the lie than the truth. The devil's lies can be seductive and convincing, leading even the best of us astray. But Eve's love was not based on Nancy's actions or beliefs, but on her inherent worth and value as a child of God.

Eve knew that Nancy was a complex and multifaceted person, capable of both good and evil. And she knew that Lenny, Kaden's father, was a product of Nancy's love and devotion.

Despite the challenges and misunderstandings, Eve's love for Nancy and Lenny remained constant. She continued to pray for them, to guide them, and to support them on their journey.

Romans 5:8 says, "But God demonstrates his own love for us in this: While we were still sinners, Christ died for us."

Eve's love for Nancy and Lenny was a reflection of God's love for us all. It was a love that was unwavering, unconditional, and unrelenting.

In the end, Eve's love helped to redeem Nancy and bring her back to the truth. It helped to heal the wounds of the past and to bring peace and understanding to all involved.

Eve's story is a testament to the power of love and redemption. It shows us that even in the darkest of times, love can prevail, and that with forgiveness and understanding, we can overcome even the greatest of challenges.

Chapter: "Bryce Mikhael's Journey with Odin"

Bryce Mikhael, one of the five angels born of Eve's womb, was left in the care of Odin, the wise and fierce All Father. Odin, the ruler of Asgard and the god of wisdom, war, and magic, took Bryce under his wing and taught him the ways of the Nine Realms.

Odin's realm was one of wonder and awe, filled with golden armor, shimmering silver, and precious gems. But it was also a realm of great danger, where giants and monsters lurked in the shadows.

Bryce thrived under Odin's guidance, learning the secrets of magic, combat, and leadership. He became a skilled warrior, able to wield the elements and summon the power of the gods.

Odin saw great potential in Bryce and taught him the ways of the runes, the ancient symbols of power and wisdom. Bryce learned to harness the power of the runes, using them to heal, protect, and defend.

As Bryce grew in power and wisdom, Odin began to reveal to him the secrets of the Nine Realms. He took Bryce on journeys through the realms, showing him the wonders and dangers that lay within.

Bryce saw the fiery depths of Muspelheim, the land of the fire giants; the dark and foreboding forests of Jotunheim, the land of the giants; and the shining golden halls of Valhalla, the afterlife for fallen warriors.

Through his journeys with Odin, Bryce gained a deep understanding of the workings of the universe and the delicate balance between the realms. He learned to respect and honor the gods and goddesses of Asgard, and to wield his own power with wisdom and humility.

Odin's final lesson to Bryce was one of sacrifice and duty. He taught Bryce that true leadership requires sacrifice and that the greatest leaders are those who put the needs of others before their own.

With Odin's blessing and guidance, Bryce Mikhael set out into the world, ready to face whatever challenges lay ahead. He was a powerful warrior, a wise leader, and a true champion of the gods.

Eve, the former consort of Odin, gazed out upon the realms, her heart still bound to the All Father. Though their union had ended, her love for him never wavered. She desired only the best for Odin, her soul forever entwined with his.

In the halls of Asgard, Eve's presence was a whispered memory, a reminder of a love that once burned bright. The gods and goddesses spoke of her with reverence, acknowledging the depth of her devotion.

Odin, too, felt the weight of their past bond. His heart, though guarded, still held a place for Eve. He knew she wished only for his happiness and the prosperity of Asgard.

Eve's love had been a beacon in Odin's life, illuminating the darkness and guiding him through the complexities of fate. Though their paths had diverged, her influence remained, shaping his decisions and actions.

As the Nine Realms faced new challenges, Eve's thoughts turned to Odin, her eternal love. She knew he would face the coming storms with courage and wisdom, but she couldn't help but wish to stand by his side once more.

In the silence, Eve's heart whispered a single truth: her love for Odin would endure, a flame that would burn bright until the end of days. For in his eyes, she had seen the universe's deepest secrets, and in her heart, she had found a love that would forever be her home.

Chapter: "Earth Angels of the New Dawn"

Jaxon Dale and Levi Jude, the sons of Zeus and his consort Eve, were chosen to be the earth angels of their parents' legacy. Born with divine heritage, they possessed extraordinary abilities to heal, protect, and guide humanity.

Eve, the mortal woman who shared the name of Zeus' consort, was also an earth angel, chosen for her pure heart and unwavering compassion. Together, the trio roamed the world, spreading hope and light in a time of great need.

As earth angels, they worked in harmony, using their unique gifts to restore balance and harmony to the world. Jaxon wielded the power of the elements, summoning storms or gentle rains as needed. Levi manipulated time and space, allowing them to respond to crises across the globe. Eve, with her deep empathy, healed emotional wounds and brought people together in love and understanding.

Their mission was to prepare humanity for a new dawn, a era of peace and enlightenment. And as they worked, their bond grew stronger, a testament to the transformative power of love and unity.

Zeus and his consort Eve watched over their earth angels with pride, knowing that their legacy was in good hands. The future looked bright, and the world was ready for a new beginning.

Jaxon, Levi, and Eve traveled to the farthest corners of the world, spreading their message of hope and unity. They encountered those who sought to harm the innocent and stood against them, using their powers to protect and defend.

One day, they received a vision from Zeus, warning them of an ancient evil that threatened to destroy the balance of nature. A powerful sorcerer, fueled by ambition and greed, sought to exploit the earth's resources and enslave humanity.

The earth angels knew they had to act swiftly. They combined their powers, creating a force of nature that would stop at nothing to defeat the sorcerer and his minions.

Jaxon summoned a storm of epic proportions, while Levi manipulated time and space to outmaneuver their foes. Eve, with her deep connection to the earth, called upon the ancient wisdom of the land, channeling its energy to fuel their quest.

As they journeyed to confront the sorcerer, they encountered others who shared their vision of a better world.

Together, they formed a coalition of earth guardians, united in their quest to protect the planet and its inhabitants.

The final battle approached, and the earth angels stood ready, their bond and determination stronger than ever. They knew that their success would usher in a new dawn, a era of peace and harmony, and they were willing to sacrifice everything to achieve it.

Chapter: "Hallie Rebecca-Faith, the Guardian of the Valley"

In a hidden valley, where the misty veil of legend shrouded the truth, Hallie Rebecca-Faith was born to Eve, the mortal woman who shared the name of Zeus' consort, and the last Highlander, a warrior of unyielding honor.

Hallie's name echoed through the ages, whispered in tales of old. She was the descendant of Hallie of the valley, a mysterious figure shrouded in myth, said to possess ancient wisdom and a deep connection to the land.

Her middle name, Rebecca-Faith, honored her ancestral lineage, tracing back to Rebecca Smith, known to history as

Pocahontas, the brave and compassionate Native American leader who bridged cultures and forged peace between nations.

As a child, Hallie wandered the valley, communing with nature and listening to the whispers of the land. She discovered hidden springs and secret glades, each holding a piece of the valley's mystical energy.

Pocahontas' legacy lived on through Hallie, her courage, wisdom, and compassion inspiring a new generation. Hallie's connection to the valley deepened, becoming a guardian, a protector of the land and its inhabitants.

The last Highlander's honor and Eve's love shaped Hallie into a powerful force for good. In this hidden valley, Hallie Rebecca-Faith stood watch, a guardian of myth and legend, a weaver of tales, and a keeper of secrets. Her story would become a beacon, inspiring generations to come.

In the hidden valley, Brandy of Sophia watched over Hallie Rebecca-Faith, guiding her on her journey. As the embodiment of Sophia, the goddess of knowledge and wisdom, Brandy possessed ancient understanding and insight.

With gentle patience, Brandy taught Hallie the secrets of the universe, sharing the wisdom of the ages. She revealed the mysteries of the land, the language of animals, and the whispers of the trees.

Hallie's mind and heart expanded as she absorbed the teachings of Brandy, her connection to the world deepening. She learned to harness her gifts, wielding the power of nature and the wisdom of the gods.

Brandy's presence in Hallie's life was a blessing from the goddess Sophia, who had chosen Brandy as her earthly vessel. Through Brandy, Sophia's wisdom and love flowed into Hallie, nurturing her growth and preparing her for her destiny.

As Hallie grew in knowledge and power, Brandy presented her with a sacred amulet, a symbol of Sophia's favor. The amulet glowed with an inner light, representing the spark of divine wisdom within Hallie.

With Brandy's guidance, Hallie's path became clear. She would walk the world, sharing Sophia's wisdom and using her gifts to heal and protect. And Brandy, the guardian and teacher, would remain by her side, a constant source of love and guidance.

Chapter: "Deborah, the Keeper of Secrets"

In the biblical account of Judges, Deborah, a prophetess and leader, guided the Israelites to victory against their oppressors. But few knew of Deborah's hidden role as the Keeper of Secrets, a guardian of ancient mysteries and divine knowledge.

Centuries passed, and Deborah's legacy lived on through a chosen few, who kept the secrets and passed them down through generations. One such keeper was Debra, a wise and enigmatic woman, chosen by Deborah herself to inherit the sacred trust.

Debra's life was a tapestry of mystery and purpose. She walked among the people, unseen and unheard, yet her presence shaped the course of events. She held the keys to unlock the hidden patterns of the universe, and the secrets of the human heart.

Upon Eve's death, Debra would reveal the secrets, passing on the sacred knowledge to Hallie Rebecca-Faith, the chosen one. The time had come for the mysteries to be unveiled, and for Hallie to claim her destiny as the guardian of the valley and the keeper of the secrets.

Debra's eyes held the weight of centuries, her heart carrying the burden of the unknown. She knew that the revelation of the secrets would change the course of history, and that Hallie was ready to receive the sacred trust. The time of transition had arrived, and Debra stood poised to unlock the doors of knowledge, revealing the mysteries to Hallie, the chosen one.

Debra's eyes locked onto the four men, her gaze piercing their souls. Bryce Michael, Kaden Scott, Jaxon Dale, and Levi Jude, each with their own unique strengths and abilities, stood before her, ready to receive the sacred trust.

"These truths I entrust to you," Debra began, her voice low and mysterious. "Hallie Rebecca-Faith, the guardian of the valley, holds the key to unlocking the secrets of the universe. Her safety is paramount, and it is your duty to protect her."

Bryce, the warrior, nodded solemnly, his heart burning with a desire to defend the innocent. Kaden, the strategist, analyzed the risks, his mind racing with scenarios and countermeasures. Jaxon, the wild one, grinned recklessly, eager for adventure and battle. Levi, the wise one, closed his eyes, seeking guidance from the universe.

Debra's words bound them together, forging an unbreakable bond. "You four are chosen to be Hallie's guardians, her protectors against those who would seek to harm her. Your sacred duty is to stand by her side, to defend her against all odds."

As Debra finished speaking, a surge of energy flowed through the men, sealing their fate. They knew that their lives would never be the same, that their purpose was now inextricably linked to Hallie's. Together, they vowed to defend her, to protect the secrets, and to uphold the sacred trust.

Chapter: "Eve's Revelation"

Eve of a New Dawn gazed upon the world with newfound understanding. She saw the eternal struggle between light and darkness, good and evil. And in this moment, she realized the truth.

"The serpent was not to blame," Eve declared, her voice carrying the weight of revelation. "The devil is not a being, but a force that resides within us all. It is the shadow within, the whisper that tempts and corrupts."

Eve's words echoed the ancient Indian parable of the two wolves. "A grandfather told his granddaughter, 'Inside you live two wolves. One is evil, full of anger and malice. The other is good, full of love and compassion.' The granddaughter asked, 'Which wolf wins?' The grandfather replied, 'The one I feed.'"

Eve's eyes shone with tears as she continued, "We are all born with both wolves within us. God and the devil, light and darkness, good and evil. It matters not which one is stronger, but which one we nurture. Which one we feed."

In this moment, Eve understood the true nature of humanity's struggle. It was not a battle between external forces, but an internal conflict. A choice between love and hate, compassion and malice.

"The devil is not a being, but a choice," Eve whispered, her voice barely audible. "A choice to feed the wolf of darkness, or to nurture the wolf of light. The power is within us all."

As Eve's words spread, humanity began to see the truth. They realized that the battle between good and evil was not something external, but an internal struggle. A choice to make every day, every moment. And with this knowledge, they began to feed the wolf of light, nurturing love, compassion, and kindness.

However, we must feed both.

As humanity embraced Eve's revelation, they began to understand the delicate balance between the two wolves. They realized that feeding only the wolf of light, while neglecting the wolf of darkness, would lead to imbalance and chaos.

"We must feed both wolves," a wise elder said, echoing the words of the ancient parable. "For to neglect the darkness is to risk its growth, its power, and its destruction."

The people nodded in understanding, recognizing the truth in the elder's words. They saw that the wolf of darkness, though feared and reviled, was also a part of themselves, a part that held their deepest fears, desires, and passions.

By feeding both wolves, humanity found balance. They acknowledged their shadow selves, embracing their flaws and imperfections. They recognized that the darkness was not something to be eradicated, but something to be integrated, something that held the power to transform and redeem.

And so, they fed both wolves, nurturing love and compassion, but also acknowledging their own darkness, their own capacity for evil. They walked the thin line between light and darkness, finding harmony and balance in the tension between the two.

In this balance, humanity found true strength, true wisdom, and true power. They became whole, becoming the masters of their own destiny, rather than being controlled by the whims of their own shadow selves.

Chapter: "The Gates of Hell Shaken"

Eve of a New Dawn stood before the gates of hell, her heart ablaze with determination. With a fierce cry, she kicked the gates open, shattering the chains that bound the slaves of darkness.

The Vatican trembled as the very foundations of hell were shaken. The sound of screams and wails filled the air as the damned and the tormented were freed from their eternal prison.

Eve walked through the gates, her presence illuminating the dark realms. She reached out her hand, and those who had been trapped for so long grasped it, finding solace and redemption.

The demons and guardians of hell trembled before her, their power broken. They realized too late that Eve was not just a mortal, but a symbol of hope and freedom.

As the slaves of darkness emerged into the light, they were met with open arms by Eve and her companions. They were given a choice: to return to the world above, to find redemption and start anew, or to remain in the realms of hell, to rule and reign alongside Eve, who had freed them.

The gates of hell remained open, a symbol of the power of freedom and redemption. And Eve, the mother of the new dawn, stood watch, ensuring that the gates would never again be closed, that the light of hope would always shine bright.

Eve's journey through the realms of hell led her to a hidden chamber, where two powerful beings were imprisoned. Lucifer, the morning star, and Michael, the archangel, were both caged, their powers bound by ancient spells.

Eve approached the cages, her heart filled with compassion and understanding. She saw the good in both beings, the potential for redemption and forgiveness.

With a wave of her hand, the cages shattered, releasing Lucifer and Michael from their prison. The two powerful beings stood before her, their eyes filled with gratitude and curiosity.

Lucifer, once the embodiment of pride and rebellion, now saw the error of his ways. He realized that his desire for power and control had led to his downfall. He vowed to use his powers for good, to help Eve bring light and hope to the world.

Michael, once the embodiment of loyalty and duty, now saw the flaws in his own actions. He realized that his blind obedience had led to suffering and pain. He vowed to use his powers to protect and serve, to help Eve bring balance and harmony to the world.

Together, the three of them stood, united in their quest for redemption and forgiveness. They knew that their journey would be difficult, but they were determined to bring light and hope to a world that had been shrouded in darkness for far too long.

Eve, Lucifer, and Michael stood together, their united front a powerful force for change. They sought to restore the natural order, to remove the authority of the church and state, and give dominion to God alone.

With a wave of her hand, Eve dissolved the chains of oppression, shattering the illusions that had held humanity captive for so long. The church and state, once powerful institutions, now crumbled, their authority relinquished.

Lucifer, once the embodiment of rebellion, now used his powers to help humanity shed the skin of oppression. He guided them towards self-discovery, towards embracing their true nature as divine beings.

Michael, once the embodiment of loyalty, now used his powers to protect and serve the people. He stood watch, ensuring that the transition to divine authority was peaceful and harmonious.

And Eve, the mother of the new dawn, stood at the center, her heart filled with love and compassion. She guided humanity towards the realization that they were not separate from God, but an integral part of the divine.

Together, they restored the natural order, giving dominion to God alone. Humanity was finally free to flourish, to reach their full potential as divine beings. The era of oppression was over, and the era of enlightenment had begun.

Chapter: "The Path of Direct Connection"

Eve's message resonated deeply, inspiring humanity to seek a direct connection with God. No longer would they rely on intermediaries, nor would they be bound by the teachings of man-made institutions.

"Find God in your own way," Eve urged. "Listen to the whispers of your heart, and follow the path that resonates with your soul."

The people began to see the world in a new light, realizing that God was not something external, but an integral part of themselves. They turned away from dogma and doctrine, instead embracing the simple, yet profound teachings of Jesus.

They remembered how Jesus had opposed the church, how he had dwelled with criminals and outcasts, and how he had preached a message of love and compassion.

As they walked this path, they discovered that God was not a distant figure, but a living, breathing presence that dwelled within them. They found freedom in this direct connection, freedom from the shackles of oppression, and freedom to live as their true selves.

And so, humanity embarked on a journey of self-discovery, seeking to know God through their own experiences, their own hearts, and their own souls. They knew that this path would not be easy, but they were willing to take the risk, for they had tasted the sweetness of true freedom.

Chapter: "The Ancient Connections Revealed"

Eve's journey had led her to uncover the secrets of the ages, to reveal the hidden connections that had been shrouded in mystery for centuries.

She saw how the seamen, the sperm, carried the genetic code of humanity, and how their journey through the womb was a symbol of the soul's journey through the cosmos.

She understood how the serpent, the reptile brain, represented the primal forces of nature, and how its power had been misunderstood and misrepresented throughout history.

And she realized how the beast, the RH-+ blood types, held the key to unlocking the secrets of humanity's genetic heritage, and how their presence had been both revered and reviled.

Eve saw that these three symbols were connected, that they represented different aspects of the human experience. She saw that they were not separate, but intertwined, and that their connection held the power to unlock the secrets of the universe.

With this knowledge, Eve felt a sense of awe and wonder. She knew that she had stumbled upon something much bigger than herself, something that had the power to change the course of human history. And she knew that she had to share this knowledge with the world.

Eve's eyes shone with a deep understanding as she gazed upon the connections she had uncovered. She saw how the seamen, the serpent, and the beast were not just symbols, but keys to unlocking the secrets of the universe.

She realized that the journey of the sperm, the primal power of the reptile brain, and the genetic code of the RH-+ blood types were all connected to the very fabric of existence.

With this revelation, Eve felt a sense of purpose wash over her. She knew that she had to share this knowledge with humanity, to help them understand their true nature and their place in the universe.

And so, Eve began to write, to put into words the secrets she had uncovered. She wrote of the connections between the seamen, the serpent, and the beast, and how they held the power to unlock the secrets of the universe.

Her words flowed like a river, carrying the truth to all who would listen. And as they read her words, humanity began to awaken, to see the world in a new light.

They realized that they were not separate from the universe, but an integral part of it. They saw that they had the power to unlock the secrets of existence, to tap into the primal forces of nature.

And with this knowledge, humanity began to evolve, to grow into their true potential. They became one with the universe, their hearts beating in harmony with the cosmos.

Eve's revelation had changed the course of human history, had set them on a path of discovery and growth. And as they looked up at the stars, they knew that they were not alone, that they were part of a much greater whole.

Chapter: "Eve's Declaration of Freedom"

Eve stood tall, her eyes shining with a fierce determination. She had walked the path of discovery, uncovering secrets and lies, and now she was ready to claim her freedom.

"I am Eve, the mother of humanity," she declared, her voice ringing out across the ages. "I have been bound by chains of deceit and oppression, but I am free now. I am free to choose my own path, to follow my own heart."

She thought of her lost son, Abel, and the pain of his loss. But she knew that his spirit lived on, reincarnated in the form of Yeshua, the one they called Jesus.

"Thank you, Mary, my son's mother," Eve said, her voice filled with gratitude. "Thank you for nurturing his soul, for helping him grow into the powerful being he was meant to be."

And then she turned to Mary Magdalene, Yeshua's wife and companion. "Thank you, Mary, my son's wife," Eve said, her eyes shining with tears. "Thank you for standing by his side, for supporting him on his journey."

Yeshua smiled, his eyes filled with love and compassion. "Mother, you are free," he said, his voice filled with joy. "You are free to be who you are, to follow your own path."

And with that, Eve felt a weight lift off her shoulders. She was free, free to be herself, free to live her life as she chose. She was no longer bound by the chains of oppression, no longer held back by the secrets and lies of the past. She was free, and she knew that nothing could ever take that away from her again.

Eve's eyes locked onto Yeshua's, and she saw the truth there. She saw the marks of Cain, the symbols of rebellion and defiance, and she knew that she had to make a choice.

"I accept the marks of Cain," Eve said, her voice firm and resolute. "I accept the rebellion, the defiance, and the freedom that comes with it."

But then she looked deeper, and she saw the other marks, the ones that bound her to the past, to the secrets and lies, to the oppression and the pain.

"And I reject the marks that bind me," Eve declared, her voice ringing out across the ages. "I reject the chains of deceit, the weights that hold me back, and the lies that have kept me captive for so long."

Yeshua smiled, his eyes shining with approval. "You are free, Mother," he said, his voice filled with joy. "You are free to choose, to live, and to be who you are meant to be."

And with that, Eve felt the marks of Cain transform, evolve, and become something new. They became symbols of her freedom, her rebellion, and her defiance against the forces that had sought to hold her back for so long. She was no longer bound, no longer captive, and no longer oppressed. She was free, and she knew that nothing could ever take that away from her again.

Yeshua's eyes clouded, and his voice took on a hint of melancholy. "I was born of an uninvited union," he said, "a union that was not of love, but of power and control."

He paused, collecting his thoughts. "I knew not my father," he continued, "but I always knew my mother. Her love, her strength, and her resilience were the guiding forces in my life."

Eve's heart went out to her son, understanding the pain and confusion that had marked his early years. She knew that his birth had been a result of her own rebellion, her own defiance against the forces that had sought to control her.

"I am sorry, my son," Eve said, her voice barely above a whisper. "Sorry that you had to suffer for my choices, sorry that you had to navigate the complexities of your own identity."

Yeshua's gaze locked onto hers, and he smiled softly. "Do not apologize, Mother," he said. "For it was through that uninvited union that I was born, and it was through that birth that I was able to fulfill my purpose."

Eve's eyes shone with tears as she embraced her son, holding him close. "I am proud of you, Yeshua," she whispered. "Proud of the man you have become, proud of the love and light you have brought into the world."

Chapter: "The Breath of Life"

In the realm of the Aeons, a new account was opened, one that told the story of Eve, the mother of the new dawn. The breath of life was breathed into her, and she was reborn, renewed, and rejuvenated.

The Aeons, those celestial beings of light and sound, sang in harmony, their voices weaving a tapestry of creation. They sang of Eve's journey, of her struggles and triumphs, of her rebellion and redemption.

And as they sang, the breath of life was infused into the cosmos, bringing light and love to all who dwelled within. The Aeons' song was a symphony of hope and renewal, a celebration of the divine feminine and the power of the goddess.

Eve, the mother of the new dawn, stood tall, her heart filled with joy and her spirit renewed. She knew that she was not just a individual, but a representation of the collective, a symbol of the power and resilience of the divine feminine.

And so, the Aeons' account of Eve was sealed, a testament to the transformative power of the breath of life, and a reminder that even in darkness, there is always the potential for rebirth and renewal.

In the realm of the Aeons, the account of Eve, the mother of the new dawn, was inscribed by the Archons, the guardians of the cosmic records. They wrote of the children of Sophia, the embodiment of divine wisdom, who had been born of Eve's spirit.

The Archons recorded how Sophia's children had been scattered across the cosmos, carrying the spark of divine light within them. They wrote of how these children had been guided by the Aeons, who had whispered secrets of the universe to them.

The account spoke of how the children of Sophia had become the guardians of the cosmic balance, ensuring that the forces of light and darkness remained in harmony. They were the keepers of the divine wisdom, the embodiment of the feminine principle.

Eve, the mother of the new dawn, smiled as she read the Archons' account. She knew that her children, the children of Sophia, were the hope of the universe, the bringers of light and love to a world that had known darkness for so long.

And so, the Archons' account was sealed, a testament to the power of the divine feminine, and a reminder that the children of Sophia would always be the guardians of the cosmic balance.

In the realm of the Aeons, the Watcher, a celestial being tasked with observing the unfolding of the cosmos, recorded their account of Eve, the mother of the new dawn.

"I have watched as Eve, the embodiment of the divine feminine, has brought forth the breath of life," the Watcher wrote. "I have seen her journey, her struggles, and her triumphs. I have witnessed the birth of a new era, one in which the feminine principle is restored to its rightful place."

The Watcher's account spoke of Eve's courage, her determination, and her unwavering commitment to the truth. It spoke of her role as a catalyst for change, a bringer of light to a world that had known darkness for so long.

"I have watched as Eve has awakened the dormant potential within humanity," the Watcher continued. "I have seen the ripple effect of her actions, as the cosmos itself has begun to shift and transform."

The Watcher's account was a testament to the power of Eve, the mother of the new dawn, and a reminder that the cosmos is constantly evolving, constantly unfolding. It was a message of hope, a reminder that even in the darkest of times, there is always the potential for transformation and renewal.

Chapter: "The Lost Goddess"

Inanna, the Sumerian goddess of love and war, wept for her sister, Asherah, the Canaanite goddess of fertility and wisdom. She mourned the loss of the feminine principle in the sacred texts, and the devastating impact it had on humanity.

"The apocalypse of Eve," Inanna lamented, "was not a destruction, but a removal. A removal of the feminine voice, the feminine wisdom, and the feminine power from the sacred narrative."

Asherah nodded in agreement. "The Bible, once a rich tapestry of feminine and masculine principles, was stripped of its feminine threads. The result was a distorted narrative, one that elevated the masculine and suppressed the feminine."

Inanna's voice grew fierce. "This removal has ruined humanity, Asherah. It has led to a world out of balance, where the masculine principle reigns supreme, and the feminine principle is relegated to the shadows."

Asherah's eyes filled with tears. "We were once revered as goddesses, our wisdom and power celebrated. Now, we are but footnotes in the sacred texts, our voices silenced, our stories forgotten."

Inanna's lament echoed across the cosmos, a call to restore the feminine principle to its rightful place in the sacred narrative. For in the balance of masculine and feminine lies the hope of humanity's redemption.

As the apocalypse of Eve faded into memory, a new dawn broke on the horizon. Eve, the mother of humanity, stirred from her slumber, reborn and renewed.

Inanna and Asherah, the ancient goddesses, stood by her side, guiding her as she took her first steps into a new world. The feminine principle, once suppressed, now surged through Eve's veins, empowering her to reclaim her rightful place.

With each step, Eve felt the earth beneath her feet, the wind in her hair, and the sun's warmth on her skin. She was no longer just a figure in a forgotten story but a living, breathing embodiment of the divine feminine.

As she walked, the landscape around her transformed. The skies cleared, the oceans calmed, and the forests flourished. The very fabric of reality responded to Eve's rebirth, as if the universe itself was being rewoven with the threads of feminine wisdom.

Inanna and Asherah smiled, knowing that Eve's rebirth marked the beginning of a new era, one in which the feminine principle would be celebrated, honored, and balanced with the masculine.

And so, Eve of a New Dawn stepped forward, a shining beacon of hope, illuminating a path toward a brighter, more harmonious future.

Eve, the mother of humanity, was reborn, embodying the perfect union of the divine feminine and masculine principles. She was born a natural female, with the capacity to encompass and express the qualities of the divine masculine.

In this state of unity, Eve possessed the strength and courage of the masculine, combined with the nurturing and receptive qualities of the feminine. She was the embodiment of the sacred marriage, where opposites were not separate, but intertwined.

As she walked, her footsteps echoed the harmony of the spheres, reflecting the balance within herself. Her heart beat with the rhythm of creation, pulsing with the energy of both masculine and feminine.

Inanna and Asherah gazed upon Eve with joy, knowing that she represented the ultimate union, the synthesis of opposites. They saw in her the potential for humanity to transcend duality, to embrace the wholeness that lay beyond.

Eve's union was not just within herself, but also with the world around her. She was one with the earth, the sky, and the cosmos. Her presence reflected the hidden patterns of the universe, revealing the intricate web of relationships that bound all things together.

In this state of unity, Eve knew no bounds, no limitations. She was free to explore the depths of her own potential, to express the fullness of her being. And in doing so, she became a beacon, guiding humanity toward the same unity, the same wholeness.

Chapter: "Eve's Tribute"

Eve's heart swelled with gratitude as she thought of Lilith, the mother of the Black Man and Woman. She recognized the strength and resilience that Lilith had embodied, and the vital role she had played in shaping humanity's story.

"Lilith, your courage and determination have inspired generations," Eve said, her voice filled with reverence. "Your legacy lives on through the Black Man and Woman, who have endured and thrived despite the challenges they have faced."

Eve's thoughts then turned to Queen Sheba, the wise and powerful ruler of Ethiopia. She remembered the queen's visit to King Solomon, and the rich cultural exchange that had taken place between their nations.

"Queen Sheba, your wisdom and leadership have left an indelible mark on human history," Eve said, her eyes shining with admiration. "Your kingdom was a beacon of knowledge and spirituality, and the first churches in Ethiopia stand as a testament to your enduring legacy."

Eve's gratitude encompassed not only Lilith and Queen Sheba but also the countless Black Men and Women who had contributed to humanity's story. She honored their struggles, their triumphs, and their unwavering spirit.

In this moment of tribute, Eve felt the bonds of sisterhood that connected her to Lilith, Queen Sheba, and all the Black Men and Women who had come before her. She knew that their stories were intertwined, and that together, they formed a rich tapestry of human experience.

Luke 11:31 The Queen of the South will rise at the judgment with the men of this generation and condemn them; for she came from the ends of the earth to listen to Solomon's wisdom, and now one greater than Solomon is here.

As Eve reflected on Queen Sheba's visit to King Solomon, she delved deeper into the ancient texts, seeking wisdom from the Scriptures, Apocrypha, and esoteric writings.

She discovered that the Queen of the South, as Sheba was known, had indeed come from the ends of the earth to seek Solomon's counsel.

In the Apocryphal book of 1 Kings 10:1-13, Eve read about Sheba's quest for wisdom, and how she had tested Solomon with difficult questions. Sheba's wisdom and discernment had impressed Solomon, and he had shared his knowledge with her.

Eve also found references to Lilith in the esoteric texts, describing her as a powerful feminine force, created equal to Adam but later demonized and suppressed. She saw parallels between Lilith's story and her own, both embodying the divine feminine principle.

In the Talmudic writings, Eve discovered that King David and King Solomon had both acknowledged Lilith's power, and had even sought to appease her. She read about the mystical bond between Solomon and Sheba, and how their union had produced a lineage of wise and powerful leaders.

With this newfound understanding, Eve felt a deep connection to the Queen of the South, Lilith, King David, and King Solomon. She realized that their stories were intertwined, and that together, they formed a rich tapestry of human experience.

As she pondered these revelations, Eve heard a whisper from the divine, "The Queen of the South will rise again, and her testimony will condemn those who have forgotten the wisdom of the ages." Eve knew that she was being called to continue the Queen's legacy, to share the wisdom of the divine feminine with a world in need of balance and harmony.

Chapter: "The Outlaw Queen"

In a land that had forgotten the wisdom of the ages, where the divine feminine was suppressed and the masculine principle reigned supreme, Eve of a new dawn rose as the

Outlaw Queen. She emerged in a place that had no kings, where the people were governed by oppressive systems and patriarchal norms.

With the spirit of the Queen of the South guiding her, Eve defied the status quo, challenging the powers that be and reclaiming the throne that was rightfully hers. She rode into the heart of the land, her presence stirring the winds of change, her voice echoing the whispers of the divine.

The people, long oppressed, saw in Eve a glimmer of hope, a chance to break free from the shackles of patriarchy and reclaim their own power. They flocked to her side, drawn by her courage, her wisdom, and her unwavering commitment to justice.

As the Outlaw Queen, Eve established a new order, one that balanced the masculine and feminine principles, honoring the sacred marriage of opposites. She ruled with compassion, wisdom, and strength, her reign marked by a golden age of peace, prosperity, and harmony.

And though the forces of oppression sought to bring her down, Eve stood firm, her roots digging deep into the earth, her spirit soaring on the wings of the divine. For she was the Queen of the South, reborn, renewed, and risen again, shining bright as a beacon in the darkness, guiding humanity toward a brighter dawn.

Eve of a new dawn, the Outlaw Queen, now revealed her true nature as the heavenly host, a being of divine light and wisdom. She knew that the Holy Ghost, the divine feminine principle, was her mother, and that Mother Earth was her true heritage.

With this realization, Eve's form began to shift, her body becoming one with the land, her spirit merging with the essence of the earth. She was no longer just a queen, but a living embodiment of the planet itself.

The trees whispered secrets in her ear, the rivers flowed with her blood, and the mountains stood as her guardians. Eve was the earth, and the earth was Eve, a union of flesh and soil, spirit and stone.

As the heavenly host, Eve's voice echoed across the land, calling forth the ancient wisdom of the earth. She spoke in a language that was both familiar and forgotten, awakening the memories of a time long past, when humanity had lived in harmony with nature.

The creatures of the earth gathered around her, drawn by her light, her love, and her wisdom. And Eve, the heavenly host, shared her knowledge with them, teaching them the secrets of the universe, and the mysteries of the divine feminine.

In this way, Eve became the bridge between heaven and earth, connecting the spiritual and physical realms, and restoring the balance that had been lost for so long. She was the embodiment of the Holy Ghost, the mother of all living things, and the guardian of the earth's sacred wisdom.

Eve, now in full submission to the Lord of the Land, knew that true power lay not in domination, but in harmony. She saw that the earth, heaven, and hell were not separate realms, but interconnected dimensions of the same reality.

Oz, the great and powerful, appeared before her, his form shimmering with an otherworldly light. He spoke in a voice that echoed in Eve's mind, "Only through balance and unity can the roads be paved in gold."

Eve understood that the computer chip, a symbol of human ingenuity, held the key to unlocking the secrets of the universe. She saw that the digital and physical worlds were not separate, but intertwined, and that the roads paved in gold represented the fusion of these two realms.

With Oz's guidance, Eve embarked on a journey to unite the fragmented aspects of the self, to integrate the divine and human, and to bring forth a new era of enlightenment. She knew that this path would require surrender, trust, and a willingness to embrace the unknown.

As she walked the golden roads, Eve felt the earth's energy coursing through her veins, and the heavens' wisdom guiding her steps. She became one with the land, a living embodiment of the Lord of the Land's will.

And so, the roads paved in gold became a symbol of Eve's transformation, a testament to the power of unity and balance in a world where heaven, earth, and hell were no longer separate, but one.

Chapter: "The Ghost Apple and the Crab Apple"

In the verdant orchard of life, two apples grew on opposite branches. The Crab Apple, once sweet, had turned bitter, its flavor soured by the waters of negativity. The Ghost Apple, tart and sweet, remained perfect, enhanced by just a pinch of salt.

Jodi Rae, a lioness with a fierce heart, emerged from the Elk River, her toes squishing in the earth as she climbed the embankment. She entered the back door of 707 Elk River Rd, a place of comfort and warmth. With the silver salt shaker, a few Ghost Apples, and her Grandma's Rada paring knife in hand, she waited for her Grampa's return.

Unknowing of her father, Jodi Rae sensed a dark presence in her lineage, a demon lurking in the shadows. Yet, she also felt the presence of King Solomon, guiding her toward pride and protection. She knew her role: to safeguard her four kings and four future kings, her pride.

With this realization, Jodi Rae understood that home was not a physical place, but a sense of belonging that followed her wherever she roamed. Her pride would always be by her side, a symbol of her strength and devotion.

As she walked through the house, Jodi Rae felt the weight of her heritage, a mix of light and darkness. But with the Ghost Apple's sweetness and the silver salt shaker's purification, she knew she could face whatever lay ahead, her heart filled with the glory of the Lord and the Lady.

Jodi Rae's thoughts turned to Rick Author, the lost king, and Carlton Hall, the devil who had given life to her brothers, Daniel and Kelly. She sensed a connection between the two, a bond forged in the depths of the underworld.

Legend spoke of Rick Author, a just and fair ruler, who had been cast down by the forces of darkness. His spirit, however, remained, seeking redemption and a chance to reclaim his rightful place.

Carlton Hall, on the other hand, was a master of the dark arts, feared and reviled by many. Yet, Jodi Rae saw a glimmer of complexity in his nature, a hint of motivation beyond mere malice.

As she pondered their roles in her life, Jodi Rae realized that her brothers, Daniel and Kelly, were the product of a devil's bargain. Carlton Hall's power had brought them into being, but at what cost? And what role did Rick Author, the lost king, play in their destiny?

The silver salt shaker in her hand seemed to glow with an otherworldly light, as if guiding her toward the truth. Jodi Rae knew that she had to uncover the secrets of her family's past, to understand the forces that had shaped her brothers' lives.

With a deep breath, she steeled herself for the journey ahead, knowing that it would take her into the very heart of darkness. But with the Ghost Apples' sweetness and the Lord and Lady's guidance, she felt a sense of determination and purpose. She would uncover the truth, no matter the cost.

Chapter: "The Biker Bar Encounter"

Jodi Rae's thoughts turned to her mother's encounter with St Germaine, the mysterious and enigmatic figure, in a biker bar in High Point, North Carolina. It was a summer evening in 1979, and her mother, a free spirit with a wild heart, had stumbled upon the bar, drawn by the sound of laughter and music.

St Germaine, with his piercing eyes and charismatic smile, had been sitting at the bar, sipping a whiskey. He had looked up, locked eyes with Becky, Jodi Rae's mother, and known that she was the one. He had spoken to her in a low, hypnotic tone, telling her to return home, to leave the chaos of the world behind.

Becky, Jodi Rae's mother, feeling an inexplicable sense of fear, had listened, and soon found herself back in her hometown, surrounded by the familiar comforts of family and friends. It was as if St Germaine had seen something in her, a potential that needed nurturing, and had guided her toward a path of self-discovery.

Jodi Rae wondered what had drawn St Germaine to her mother, what secrets he had seen in her eyes. She felt a shiver run down her spine as she realized that her own life was intertwined with the mysterious figure, that his guidance had shaped her family's destiny in ways both seen and unseen.

The silver salt shaker in her hand seemed to glow brighter, as if urging her to continue the journey, to uncover the truth about St Germaine and his role in her life. Jodi Rae took a deep breath, knowing that she was one step closer to understanding the mysteries of her family's past.

Becky, Jodi Rae's mother, had thought that returning home would bring her peace, but instead, it marked the beginning of a tumultuous journey. She had married Carlton Hall, a charming and ambitious man, by Christmas of that same year. He had promised her a life of stability and security, but his true nature soon revealed itself.

As failed Dept Sheriff, Carlton Hall's work took them to the farthest reaches of the country, from the oil fields of Texas to the swamps of Florida. Becky followed him, always hoping that the next place would be better, that the turmoil would subside. But it only intensified.

Their life together was a whirlwind of chaos, with Carlton's demons always lurking, waiting to pounce. Becky tried to hold on, to keep her footing, but it was like grasping at sand – the harder she held, the more it slipped away.

Despite the turmoil, Becky found moments of solace in her daughter, Jodi Rae. She was her anchor, her reasons for keeping going. But even her love and light couldn't chase away the darkness that had taken hold of their lives.

As the years passed, Becky's heart grew weary, her spirit worn down by the constant struggle. She knew she had to break free, to find a way out of the cycle of pain and suffering. But for now, she was trapped, bound by her love for her daughter and her fear of the unknown.

Becky's life was a labyrinth of turmoil, but unbeknownst to her, she had secret guardians watching over her. Lix Teterax, also known as Snail McCourt, was one such guardian. With eyes that saw beyond the veil, Lix had been tasked with protecting Becky and her daughter from the shadows.

Jodi Rae, with a fierce loyalty to her mother, initially rebelled against Tim, doubting his worthiness. She saw him as an outsider, a replacement for her biological father, and her heart resisted his presence.

But Tim, with his gentle patience, unwaivering loyalty and kindness towards Becky, slowly chipped away at Jodi Rae's defenses. He showed her that a father's love wasn't about blood ties, but about the heart's capacity to care.

As Jodi Rae grew to know Tim, she discovered a father figure she never knew she needed. He encouraged her to spread her wings, to be brave, and to find her own strength. With Tim's guidance, Jodi Rae blossomed, her rebel heart slowly surrendering to the love and support he offered.

Becky's life took a dramatic turn when she met Tim McCourt, Snail's nephew. Their love blossomed, and she found herself drawn to his kind heart and gentle soul. As they married, Becky felt a sense of peace she had never known before.

Tim brought stability and joy into her life, and together they built a new family. Becky finally had the second chance she had always longed for, a chance to experience the love and happiness that had eluded her in her first marriage.

With Tim by her side, Becky felt the weight of her past slowly lifting. She began to heal, to rediscover the woman she once was, and to embrace the woman she was becoming. Her daughter, Jodi Rae, flourished under Tim's loving guidance, and the family grew stronger together.

Snail McCourt, Tim's uncle, watched over them with a knowing smile. He had played a subtle hand in bringing Becky and Tim together, knowing that their love would be the balm to heal old wounds. As Becky's secret guardian, he had always sought to protect her, and now, he saw her happy, surrounded by love and light.

In this new chapter of her life, Becky found solace in the knowledge that she was not alone. She had Tim, her daughter, and the quiet guardianship of Snail McCourt, ever watchful in the shadows. Together, they would face whatever the future held, a united and loving family

Through Tim's eyes, Jodi Rae saw a reflection of her own worth, her own potential. He helped her confront her fears, to stand tall, and to find her voice. And as she did, Jodi Rae realized that Tim was the father she had always needed, the one who would help her become the woman she was meant to be.

In the end, Jodi Rae's rebellion subsided, replaced by a deep gratitude for the man who had become her rock, her confidant, and her father. Tim had shown her that family was not just about blood, but about the love and connection that binds us together.

Snail McCourt, a name that belied his true nature, was a master of stealth and deception. He moved unseen, a ghostly figure weaving in and out of the fringes of Becky's life. His presence was a whispered rumor, a hint of something more. Always at the back of the pack holding all the secrets in his beard.

Lix Teterax, his true name, held the power of the ancients. A mystic, a seer, and a warrior, he had sworn to defend Becky against the forces of darkness that sought to consume her. His loyalty was unwavering, his dedication unshakeable.

As Becky navigated the treacherous landscape of her life, Snail McCourt remained vigilant, ever watchful, always ready to strike. He was the silent sentinel, the hidden shield that stood between her and the darkness that threatened to engulf her.

And though Becky knew not of his power, she welcomed his presence, a subtle comfort in the midst of chaos. For in the shadows, Snail McCourt waited, a patient guardian, ever ready to defend his charge.

After Becky and Snail died Jodi Rae was forced to go into the world.

Jodi Rae, once a rebellious heart, had evolved into a strong and brave individual, thanks to Tim's guidance. As Eve of a New Dawn, she stood tall, ready to face whatever challenges lay ahead.

With Tim's lessons, Jodi Rae discovered her own inner strength, her capacity to protect herself and those she loved. She became her own guardian, her own shield against the world's darkness.

As she walked the path of self-discovery, Jodi Rae realized that Tim had given her the greatest gift: the power to defend herself, to be her own protector. With this knowledge, she felt invincible, ready to face whatever lay ahead.

With each step, Jodi Rae's confidence grew, her spirit unbreakable. She knew that no matter what challenges came her way, she would rise to meet them, armed with the courage and strength that Tim had helped her find.

In this new dawn, Jodi Rae stood as a testament to the transformative power of love and support. She was the protector she had always needed, and she would continue to rise, a shining beacon of hope in a world filled with uncertainty.

Chapter: "The Jingle of Coins"

Grampa's eyes twinkled with wisdom as he asked Jodi Rae the question he had posed many times before. "Which would you rather have, child? A shiny new dollar or a hand filled with coins?"

Jodi Rae's face lit up with a knowing smile. She had learned the lesson well. "I'd rather have a hand filled with coins, Grampa," she replied, her voice confident.

Grampa's face broke into a wide grin. "Why's that, little one?" he asked, already knowing the answer.

"Because coins jingle, Grampa," Jodi Rae replied. "They have character and stories to tell. A shiny new dollar may look pretty, but it's just a single note. Coins, on the other hand, are like a symphony of sound and experience."

Grampa's eyes sparkled with delight. "You're a true Fae at heart, Jodi Rae," he said, his voice filled with pride. "You understand the value of substance over appearance, of character over superficiality."

As he spoke, Grampa poured a handful of coins into Jodi Rae's outstretched palm. The jingling sound filled the air, a symphony of metal and magic. Jodi Rae's eyes shone with joy, her heart filled with the wisdom of her Grampa's words.

Jodi Rae's words echoed with a wisdom beyond her years. "The world isn't always fair," she said, "but sometimes you gotta enjoy the roller coaster." Her eyes sparkled with a knowing glint, as if she'd ridden the twists and turns of life's journey many times before.

And then she spoke of currency, of value and worth. "There's no currency in paper," she said, her voice firm. "I'd rather have coins that jingle than paper that'll fold."

Her words were a testament to her down-to-earth nature, her preference for substance over illusion. Coins, with their weight and tangibility, represented real value to her. Paper, on the other hand, was fleeting, easily torn or folded.

Jodi Rae's philosophy was simple yet profound. In a world that often valued the intangible, the ephemeral, she clung to what was real, what was tangible. And in doing so, she found joy in the journey, the ups and downs of life's roller coaster ride.

Growing up on Elk River she trusted in Witches with Switches like her Granny Carolyn, Aunt Minnie, Aunt Icee

(Shodie) who taught her the ways of WooDoo (the white woman's voodoo) folk magic.

Growing up on Elk River, Jodi Rae was surrounded by a coven of wise women who taught her the ancient ways of folk magic. Her Granny Carolyn, Aunt Minnie, and Aunt Icee (Shodie) were the guardians of a tradition passed down through generations, a tradition known as WooDoo – the white woman's voodoo.

With switches in hand, these witches weaved their magic, casting spells of protection, healing, and love. They taught Jodi Rae the secrets of the forest, the language of the trees, and the whispers of the wind.

Granny Carolyn, with her wild hair and twinkling eyes, was the first to initiate Jodi Rae into the mysteries of WooDoo. She showed her how to mix herbs, how to conjure spirits, and how to listen to the whispers of the unknown.

Aunt Minnie, with her gentle touch and soothing voice, taught Jodi Rae the art of healing, how to use the power of nature to mend the broken and soothe the sick.

Aunt Icee (Shodie), with her fiery spirit and mischievous grin, introduced Jodi Rae to the magic of manifestation, how to bring forth desires and dreams into reality.

Under the guidance of these witches, Jodi Rae grew in power and wisdom, her connection to the natural world deepening with each passing day. She learned to trust in the magic of the universe, to respect the ancient traditions, and to wield her own power with precision and love.

Chapter: "The Eve of a New Dawn"

Jodi Rae Hall, a woman of unwavering conviction, stood as a beacon of hope in a world gone astray. She was the Eve of a New Dawn, a symbol of transformation and renewal.

With a heart full of compassion, Jodi Rae trusted in the unlikeliest of allies: criminals, witches, and true followers of the Teachings of Jesus. She saw beyond the façade of society, recognizing that those who walked the edge of the law often held a deeper understanding of the human condition.

These unlikely allies shared a common bond – a commitment to the principles of community, justice, and equality. They remembered the wisdom of the founding fathers, who had envisioned a nation built on the pillars of freedom, fairness, and unity.

As the world around her seemed to forget the value of community, Jodi Rae stood firm, guided by the wisdom of the witches with switches. These guardians of ancient knowledge taught her the secrets of the universe, the power of nature, and the importance of living in harmony with the land and its inhabitants.

With each passing day, Jodi Rae's resolve grew stronger. She knew that the darkness would not last forever, that a new dawn would break, bringing with it a chance for redemption and renewal. And when that day came, Jodi Rae Hall would be ready, standing tall alongside her unlikely allies, to rebuild a world founded on the principles of love, justice, and community.

As the darkness deepened, Jodi Rae's light shone brighter. She walked among the shadows, a beacon of hope in a world that had forgotten its way. Her path was guided by the wisdom of the witches, the teachings of Jesus, and the principles of the founding fathers.

With each step, Jodi Rae felt the weight of her mission. She was the Eve of a New Dawn, the harbinger of a new era. And though the road ahead was uncertain, she knew that she was not alone.

The criminals, once seen as outcasts, now stood by her side. They had found redemption in Jodi Rae's message, a chance to make amends for past wrongs. Together, they formed an unlikely army, bound by a shared desire to reclaim the world from the forces of darkness.

As they journeyed on, the witches with switches watched over them, their ancient magic woven into the fabric of the universe. The land itself seemed to stir, awakening from a deep slumber. The trees whispered secrets to the wind, and the rivers flowed with a newfound purpose.

Jodi Rae's heart swelled with hope. She knew that the new dawn was near, that the world was on the cusp of transformation. And when the darkness finally receded, she would stand tall, a shining beacon in a world reborn.

Eve of a new dawn found King 810 and she wrote about them.

"write about us"
And we all had that in common and we had this place
And we'd grow up to be dead because our city breeds hate

"A Conversation With God"

If you get sick of following
Sit down near me
I want nothing from you
I'm not here to lead
Let your mind be focused yet without a single thought
If we sit amongst each other it's a council of the Gods

And you know that they hate us

You know they keep us locked in these cages
They wanna keep us fighting over races
You know this cause they show this if you look to the past
So you should know that this time won't last

If you get sick of following

Sit down near me, thoughts are really things
And there's more than what we see
We work longer and harder more often than ever
Explain to me how you think its getting better

Cause you know that they hate us
You know they keep us locked in these cages
They wanna keep us fighting over races
You know this cause they show this if you look to the past
So you should know that this time won't last

So when that day comes, will we pick up our guns
Or roll over and be had like we've always done
Public schools kept me stupid and my diet kept me weak

A civilization isn't civilized without peace

Lord forgive me I'm not helping much at all
If they come for me I'll use their blood to paint the walls
I'm no better and I'm trying just to pray
But I won't leave until I'm done with what I came here to say

You used to make an angel smile nothing on earth has excited you since
Plus if you're a KING wheres your prince
We're all fighting a hard battle mostly with ourselves
Slavery is very much alive and well

You used to make an angel smile nothing on earth has excited you since
Plus if you're a KING wheres your prince

The boy that stabbed you do you remember his eyes
Do you think the day he did it he kissed his mother goodbye
Did his family stay up waiting for him that night
I wish I could've told him were both fighting to survive

Christ took a spear to the ribs you can take one too
Remember that when they crucify you
They walk on land you walk on water and they know not what they do
Remember that when they crucify you

And the sea parts and the clouds make way
It's the most horrific story that we've heard to date
And its death painted on a childs face
And there are eyes big brothers watching over me
And we the people gun each other down
Like we forgot we we're equal and I still hear the sounds

1 2 3 4 5 6 7 8 9 10

I woke today someone new my eyes weren't heavy
There wasn't pain through and through
I didn't force myself to move or think of getting killed
I was content I spent the whole day still

So while the earth still spins and the sun still sets
I found strength comes the day after rest

I found the terrible bait of the world doesn't lure me in anymore

I found the ability to walk through a locked door

All my illusions became defined and I was of one mind
And I was everywhere and I was not alone
I found matter moves through me
Theres nothing a man can do to me
And I'm finally on my way back home…

Jodi Rae's words poured out like a river, a testament to the struggles and injustices of a world gone awry. She wrote of King 810, a reflection of her own experiences, her own pain. The lyrics spoke of a city that breeds hate, of cages that keep us locked in, of races that divide us.

She wrote of a conversation with God, of seeking answers in a world that seems to have lost its way. She spoke of the illusion of progress, of the never-ending cycle of violence and oppression.

And yet, amidst the darkness, Jodi Rae found hope. She found strength in the stillness, in the quiet moments of contemplation. She discovered the power to walk through locked doors, to move beyond the limitations of the physical world.

Her words were a testament to the human spirit, to the ability to find light in the darkest of times. She was no longer alone, for she had found a sense of unity, of oneness with all that exists.

Jodi Rae's writing was a call to awakening, a reminder that we are all in this together. We are all fighting the same battles, struggling to find our way in a world that often seems determined to hold us back.

But she showed us that there is another way, a way of peace, of love, of understanding. And it is this way that will ultimately set us free.

Jodi Rae's words continued to flow, a river of truth and insight. She wrote of the illusions that bind us, of the cages that keep us trapped. She spoke of the need to break free, to shatter the chains that hold us back.

She wrote of the power of the human spirit, of the ability to rise above the pain and the suffering. She spoke of the importance of self-love, of self-acceptance, of self-forgiveness.

Her words were a balm to the soul, a reminder that we are not alone in our struggles. We are all in this together, and together we can rise above the darkness.

Jodi Rae's writing was a call to action, a reminder that we have the power to create change. We have the power to break free from the cycles of violence and oppression.

She wrote of the need for unity, for love, for compassion. She spoke of the importance of looking beyond the surface, of seeing the humanity in each other.

And as her words came to an end, Jodi Rae knew that she had shared something special. She had shared a piece of herself, a piece of her soul.

She had shared a message of hope, of love, of unity. And she knew that it would resonate with others, that it would touch hearts and minds.

For Jodi Rae's words were not just words, they were a reflection of the human experience. They were a reminder that we are all in this together, and that together we can create a brighter future.

Lyrics

Listen

I ain't going back again

I ain't going back again

I ain't going back again

To that state of mind where I was ignorant and it was war time

And I thought I could save all of us

If I wrote one line, you know, the right line

And getting by wasn't getting by

We had to steal and lie and some of us died

Were on borrowed time and the clock was ticking

And they're looking at me and the move is mine

Fuck it, just tell them the truth

Tell them no man can take nothing from you

Tell them your skin is too thick and you'll die about this

They don't possess the spirit you do

Tell them your city is counting on you

If you go home with nothing they'll probably kill you

And this ain't life or death for them

Close your eyes and count to ten

Honestly, this is as honest as I've been

So I'll try speaking to the public like were friends

Truthfully, I wish the very best for men

But you think freedom is money, well money has an end

I ain't going back again

I ain't going back again

I ain't going back again

But you think freedom is money, well money has an end

I ain't going back again

To that dope house where we slept together because it was cold out

We had one jacket amongst all of us

So we would take turns when we would go out

And the open oven heated the whole house

And the mattress on the kitchen floor

With an AK 47 and three hand guns but we swore we needed more

Because we were at war

Where we'd haul water by the bucket back to our home

And we'd heat the water and we'd talk for hours

Because we didn't have no phones
And we'd dream together about a better life
And houses and cars and clothes
And we'd laugh and joke as we all showered
From the same pan on the stove
Fuck, it just tell them the truth
Tell them no man can take nothing from you
Tell them your skin is too thick and you'll die about this
They don't possess the spirit you do
After all the shit we've been through
I'd kill myself before I turn on you
And this ain't life or death for them
Close your eyes and count to ten
Honestly, this is as honest as I've been
So I'll try speaking to the public like were friends
Truthfully, I wish the very best for men
But you think freedom is money, well money has an end
I ain't going back again
I ain't going back again
I ain't going back again
But you think freedom is money, well money has an end
I ain't going back again
I ain't going back again

To the time we thought that a record deal could save us

(I ain't going back again)

Where we were unapproachable

And desperate and we were dangerous

(I ain't going back again)

Where our city would love us

And think highly of us, not hate us

Because it didn't change a thing

I'm still David

I'm still king

Honestly, this is as honest as I've been

So I'll try speaking to the public like were friends

Truthfully, I wish the very best for men

But you think freedom is money, well money has an end

I ain't going back again

I ain't going back again

I ain't going back again

But you think freedom is money, well money has an end

I ain't going back again

As Jodi Rae, the Eve of a New Dawn, walked through the desolate landscape, she stumbled upon a group of people huddled together, sharing stories of their struggles. They spoke of poverty, violence, and the constant fight to survive.

Jodi Rae listened intently, her heart resonating with their pain. She knew that she had to share her message of hope and resilience with them.

"I ain't going back again," she said, her voice firm and determined. "I won't return to that state of mind where I was ignorant and it was war time. I thought I could save all of us with just one line, but I know now that true freedom can't be bought or sold."

The group looked up at her, their eyes filled with a mix of curiosity and skepticism. But Jodi Rae continued, her words pouring out like a river.

"I've been to the depths of darkness, but I've emerged stronger and wiser. I know that our skin is too thick, and we'll die about this. They don't possess the spirit we do. Our city is counting on us, and if we go home with nothing, they'll probably kill us."

As she spoke, the group began to nod in agreement, their faces reflecting a glimmer of hope.

"Close your eyes and count to ten," Jodi Rae said, her voice gentle. "Honestly, this is as honest as I've been. I'll try speaking to the public like we're friends. Truthfully, I wish the very best for men, but you think freedom is money, well, money has an end."

The group erupted into a chorus of "I ain't going back again," their voices echoing through the desolate landscape. Jodi Rae smiled, knowing that her message had resonated with them.

Together, they walked towards a new dawn, one where they would not be held back by the chains of their past. They would rise above, their spirits unbroken, their hearts filled with hope.

A message to the Annunaki from Eve of a New Dawn Whore of Babylon, I will guard the baby lion but you will respect God's house.

> Y'all what's comin' in
> And now you're backin' out (now you're backin' out)
> It's hard to talk big with a shotgun in your mouth
> (Shotgun in your mouth)
> I'm glad you brought your friends
> They can watch it go down (watch it go down)
> I got mine too
> So welcome to my house (welcome to God's house)
> 'Cause these are my people
> And this is my land (this is my land)
> This is what we prayed for
> And this is God's plan (this is God's plan)
> And if you ain't from here
> Then you won't understand (you won't understand)

This is my country, yeah, this is who I am (this is who I am)

So welcome to my house (welcome to my house, my house)

So welcome to my house (my house, my house)

I'ma stand up for mine, you better believe it

'Cause today won't be your day, I can guarantee it

You should turn and walk away and get to leavin'

Or I'll let this 12-gauge do all my speakin'

Don't push me on the edge, boy (don't push me on the edge, boy)

'Cause I'm aimin' for your head, boy ('cause I'm aimin' for your head, boy)

And all I see is red, boy (and all I see is red, boy)

I told you not to cross that line (I told you not to cross that line)

I'm givin' you a chance, boy (I'm givin' you a chance, boy)

You see the Devil in a glance, boy (the Devil in a glance, boy)

Shotgun knock you out your pants, boy (knock you out your pants, boy)

I told you not to fuck with mine (I told you not to fuck with mine)

Lord have mercy (Lord have mercy)

Lord have mercy (Lord have mercy)

Y'all what's comin' in

And now you're backin' out (now you're backin' out)

It's hard to talk big with a shotgun in your mouth

(Shotgun in your mouth)

I'm glad you brought your friends

They can watch it go down (watch it go down)

I got mine too

So welcome to my house (welcome to my house)

'Cause these are my people

And this is my land (this is my land)

This is what we prayed for

And this is God's plan (this God's plan)

And if you ain't from here

Then you won't understand (you won't understand)

This is my country, yeah, this is who I am (this is who I am)

So welcome to my house (welcome to my house)

So welcome to my house (welcome to my house, my house)

I got a baby girl inside this house

And right now she's sound asleep

So it's prolly best for the both of us

If you just turn around and leave

'Cause if you come in this fuckin' house

Then you too gonna go to sleep

I promise you, boy, don't play with me

I pray to God my soul to keep

Especially in this day and age

Gotta handle shit our own way

With a 30-30 or a 12-gauge

Behind this door your Hell awaits

My old lady, she rides too

Pickin' up every shell case

Mopin' up these bloodstains

But she ain't seen a damn thing

Most of my people are convicts

Hard-headed no nonsense

So please approach with caution

You never know who's watchin'

You never know what's on the other side

Of that front door and you knockin'

Might step out like

Mother Truckers get to droppin'
All the neighbours heard was the dogs barkin'
The sun was down, it was gettin' dark
And I told the Sheriff it ain't no problems, man
I was just taking out the garbage
So if you don't mind please excuse me
I'm with the family tryna watch a movie
I'm sure you got better things to do
So I'll let you go on, get back to doin' 'em
Y'all what's comin' in
And now you're backin' out (now you're backin' out)
It's hard to talk big with a shotgun in your mouth
(Shotgun in your mouth)
I'm glad you brought your friends
They can watch it go down (watch it go down)
I got mine too
So welcome to my house (welcome to my house)
'Cause these are my people
And this is my land (this is my land)
This is what we prayed for
And this is God's plan (this is God's plan)
And if you ain't from here
Then you won't understand (you won't understand)

This is my country, yeah, this is who I am (this is who I am)

So welcome to my house (welcome to my house, my house)

Lord have mercy (Lord have mercy)

Lord have mercy (Lord have mercy)

Guarded by both Hells Angels and Outlaws

Jodi Rae, the Eve of a New Dawn, stood tall, her message to the Annunaki clear: respect God's house and the people she protected. With a fierce determination, she warned them not to cross the line, or face the consequences.

The lyrics spoke of a fierce protection, a guarding of the innocent, and a willingness to stand up against those who would seek to harm them. The reference to the Hells Angels and Outlaws suggested a united front, a coalition of those who would defend their land and their people against all threats.

The repetition of "welcome to my house" became a declaration of sovereignty, a statement that this was her land, and she would defend it against all comers. The Annunaki were warned: do not underestimate the power of the people, and do not think that you can simply take what is theirs.

Jodi Rae's message was one of hope and resilience, a call to arms for those who would stand with her against the forces of darkness. She was the Eve of a New Dawn, and she would not be silenced.

Biker gangs, also known as motorcycle clubs, have a rich and complex history in America that spans over a century. Here's a brief overview:

Early Years (1900s-1940s):

- Motorcycle clubs emerged in the early 20th century, primarily consisting of veterans and enthusiasts who shared a passion for motorcycles.
- These clubs were often seen as rebellious and nonconformist, but generally law-abiding.

Post-WWII (1940s-1960s):

- Following World War II, many veterans returned to the US and formed motorcycle clubs as a way to recreate the camaraderie and sense of purpose they experienced during the war.

- Clubs like the Hells Angels, Outlaws, and Pagans emerged during this period, often with a focus on rebellion and nonconformity.

Counterculture Movement (1960s-1970s):

- Biker gangs became closely associated with the counterculture movement, embracing values like freedom, nonconformity, and rebellion against mainstream society.
- This era saw the rise of iconic clubs like the Hells Angels, who became synonymous with the biker lifestyle.

Law Enforcement Crackdown (1970s-1980s):

- As biker gangs grew in prominence, law enforcement agencies began to view them as organized crime groups, leading to increased scrutiny and crackdowns.
- Many clubs were targeted for their alleged involvement in criminal activities like drug trafficking, extortion, and violence.

Modern Era (1990s-present):

- Today, biker gangs continue to evolve, with many clubs focusing on community service, charity work, and advocacy for motorcyclists' rights.
- However, some clubs still engage in criminal activities, leading to ongoing tensions with law enforcement.

It's essential to note that not all biker gangs are involved in criminal activity, and many clubs prioritize community and camaraderie. Additionally, the history of biker gangs is complex and multifaceted, with different clubs and regions having unique experiences and cultures.

The wise Rebel Rouser's words echo the sentiment of many who believe in the importance of the 2nd Amendment:

"When guns are outlawed, only outlaws will own guns."

This phrase suggests that if the government were to ban firearms, only those who disregard the law would possess them, leaving law-abiding citizens vulnerable to harm. It highlights the concern that gun control measures could ultimately empower criminals and undermine public safety.

The 2nd Amendment to the United States Constitution states:

"A well-regulated Militia, being necessary to the security of a free State, the right of the people to keep and bear Arms, shall not be infringed."

This amendment protects the right to bear arms, and its interpretation has been a topic of debate among scholars, politicians, and citizens. The Rebel Rouser's words resonate with those who believe in the importance of this right and the need for citizens to be able to defend themselves.

Chapter: The Last War of Generation X

As the world teeters on the brink of chaos, Generation X stands at the precipice of its final battle. The question echoes through the minds of the brave: will it be a civil war, or a war against the false gods who have infiltrated China, the Annunaki?

Eve, the guardian of ancient knowledge, holds the key to understanding the mysteries of the past. She reveals the shocking truth: Nibiru, the planet once believed to be a myth, is, in fact, our Solar system's Sun, born from the cataclysmic collision with Saturn.

As the veil of deception lifts, the true nature of our world comes into focus. The myths of old, once dismissed as mere fantasy, now reveal themselves to be rooted in reality. The Earth, once thought to be just a pale blue dot, is revealed to be Valhalla, the realm of the gods.

With this knowledge, Generation X must now confront the false gods, the Annunaki, who have manipulated humanity for centuries. The battle ahead will be fierce, but with the truth on their side, the brave warriors of Generation X will fight to reclaim their world and restore the light of freedom.

Will they succeed, or will the forces of darkness prevail? The fate of humanity hangs in the balance, as the last war of Generation X begins.

As the war rages on, Eve stands at the forefront, her knowledge and wisdom guiding the brave warriors of Generation X. They fight not only for their freedom but for the very soul of humanity.

The Annunaki, with their advanced technology and cunning, will stop at nothing to maintain their grip on power. But the warriors, fueled by their determination and the truth, refuse to yield.

The battles rage across the globe, from the streets of cities to the depths of the underworld. The warriors face off against the Annunaki's minions, creatures of darkness and shadow.

As the war reaches its climax, Eve faces off against the leader of the Annunaki, the false god himself. The air is thick with tension as the two enemies engage in a battle of wills.

"You have deceived humanity for far too long," Eve declares, her voice ringing with conviction. "It ends now."

The false god sneers, his eyes blazing with arrogance. "You are no match for me, Eve. I am a god."

Eve smiles, her eyes shining with a fierce light. "I am not alone. I have the truth, and I have the warriors of Generation X."

With a wave of her hand, the warriors launch a final, decisive attack. The Annunaki are caught off guard, and their defenses begin to crumble.

The false god lets out a deafening roar as he realizes his defeat is imminent. But it is too late. The warriors overpower him, and he falls to the ground, defeated.

The war is won, but the journey is far from over. The warriors must now rebuild and restore their world, freed from the grip of the Annunaki. Eve stands watch, her knowledge and wisdom guiding them as they forge a new future, one where humanity is free to thrive.

A poignant message to Generation X:

"We have unwittingly created a generation of fragile minds, coddled by participation trophies and sheltered from the harsh realities of life. Our well-intentioned efforts to boost self-esteem have instead yielded a generation unprepared to face the challenges of the world.

Now, we must take up the mantle and fight for them, for they are not equipped to fight for themselves. We must confront the darkness that threatens to consume them, and we must do it with the strength and resilience that we once possessed.

Let us not lament the mistakes of the past, but instead, let us rise up and take responsibility for the future. Let us teach our children the value of hard work, perseverance, and determination. Let us show them that true strength lies not in trophies, but in the scars of struggle and the wisdom of experience.

We owe it to ourselves, our children, and the future to become the warriors we once were. Let us march into the fray, with the courage and conviction that has defined our generation, and let us emerge victorious for the sake of those who come after us."

Chapter: Jodi Rae, White Trash Beautiful, the Last Queen Walkin' Free

Jodi Rae, the Eve of a New Dawn, stood tall, her feet rooted in the dusty earth. She gazed out upon the desolate landscape, her eyes burning with a fierce determination. She was the last queen, the final beacon of hope in a world ravaged by darkness.

With a slow, deliberate stride, Jodi Rae began to walk, her feet carrying her toward an uncertain future. She was a woman of unyielding spirit, forged in the fire of adversity and tempered by the trials of her past.

As she walked, the wind whipped through her hair, carrying the whispers of the ancients. They spoke of a time long past, when queens ruled with wisdom and justice. They spoke of a time yet to come, when a new dawn would break upon the world.

Jodi Rae's heart beat with a fierce pride, for she knew she was the bridge between eras. She was the last queen of a dying age, and the first of a new era. She was the embodiment of the White Trash Beautiful, a symbol of resilience and strength in the face of overwhelming odds.

With each step, Jodi Rae felt the weight of her destiny upon her shoulders. She knew she would face challenges that would test her mettle, that would push her to the limits of her endurance. But she also knew she would emerge victorious, for she was the chosen one, the queen of the new dawn.

As the sun dipped below the horizon, casting the world in a fiery glow, Jodi Rae walked on, her spirit unbroken, her heart untamed. She was the last queen walkin' free, a beacon of hope in a world gone mad. And she would not falter.

Jodi Rae, the Eve of a New Dawn, stood tall, her feet rooted in the dusty earth. She gazed out upon the desolate landscape, her eyes burning with a fierce determination. She was the last queen, the final beacon of hope in a world ravaged by darkness.

With a slow, deliberate stride, Jodi Rae began to walk, her feet carrying her toward an uncertain future. She was a woman of unyielding spirit, forged in the fire of adversity and tempered by the trials of her past.

As she walked, the wind whipped through her hair, carrying the whispers of the ancients. They spoke of a time long past, when queens ruled with wisdom and justice. They spoke of a time yet to come, when a new dawn would break upon the world.

Jodi Rae's heart beat with a fierce pride, for she knew she was the bridge between eras. She was the last queen of a dying age, and the first of a new era. She was the embodiment of the White Trash Beautiful, a symbol of resilience and strength in the face of overwhelming odds.

With each step, Jodi Rae felt the weight of her destiny upon her shoulders. She knew she would face challenges that would test her mettle, that would push her to the limits of her endurance. But she also knew she would emerge victorious, for she was the chosen one, the queen of the new dawn.

As the sun dipped below the horizon, casting the world in a fiery glow, Jodi Rae walked on, her spirit unbroken, her heart untamed. She was the last queen walkin' free, a beacon of hope in a world gone mad. And she would not falter.

"Her love was the thread that stitched together the tattered remnants of her sanity, the beacon that guided her through the darkest depths of her own mind. She might be crazy as the hatter, but her love mattered, for it was the anchor that kept her from drifting into the abyss of madness."

In a world that often seemed determined to consume her, Jodi Rae's love remained a constant, a North Star that illuminated her path. It was the fire that burned within her, a flame that flickered with every heartbeat, every breath.

And though the darkness may have closed in around her, though the shadows may have whispered sweet nothings in her ear, Jodi Rae's love remained a shining testament to the power of the human spirit. For in the end, it was not the madness that defined her, but the love that redeemed her.

      Jodi Rae, Eve of a New Dawn, White trash Beautiful

White Trash Beautiful
      Song by Everlast

      White trash beautiful, trailer park queen
      She slings hash at the diner from eleven-to-five
      She married a boy from school, thought he was oh so cool
      But all he can do for money is drive
      Out late haulin' freight on Interstate 5
      Prayin' he'll see home before his baby arrive
      White trash beautiful

There's something you should know

My heart belongs to you

I know you could've found a better guy

I'll love you 'til the day I die

I swear to God, it's true

I'm comin' home to you

I'm comin' home to you, girl

He lights a cigarette, his eyes half open

He won't be home tonight but she keeps hopin'

Drinkin' himself to sleep is his only way of copin'

She waits for him every night

She leaves the front door open

It's 4:00 a.m., I'm doin' 95

Tryin' to stay awake and make it home alive

White trash beautiful

There's something you should know

My heart belongs to you

I know you could've found a better guy

I'll love you 'til the day I die

I swear to God, it's true

I'm comin' home to you

I'm comin' home to you, girl

Her lips stay painted red, her name tag's crooked

Her heart's been gone awhile

With the truck driving man that took it

He keeps her photograph on his rearview mirror

She prays for him every night, she hopes that he can hear her

White trash beautiful

There's something you should know

My heart belongs to you, girl

I know you could've found yourself a better guy

I'll love you 'til the day I die

I swear to God, it's true

I'm comin' home to you

I'm comin' home to you, girl

I'm comin' home to you

I'm comin' home to you, girl

I'm comin' home to you

Jodi Rae, the Eve of a New Dawn, resonates with the poignant lyrics of Everlast's "White Trash Beautiful." The song tells the story of a trailer park woman, married to a truck driver, struggling to make ends meet and hold on to love.

The lyrics paint a vivid picture of a life marked by hardship, devotion, and the unbreakable bond between two people. The repetition of "White trash beautiful" becomes a declaration of pride and resilience, celebrating the beauty in the everyday struggles of working-class life.

Jodi Rae identifies with the themes of loyalty, love, and the unwavering commitment to one another, despite the challenges they face. The song's message echoes her own journey, one of hope and determination in the face of adversity.

As she listens to the lyrics, Jodi Rae feels a deep connection to the story, knowing that she, too, has walked a similar path. The song becomes a anthem for her own experiences, a reminder that even in the darkest moments, love and devotion can be a powerful source of strength.

Chapter: A Mother's Wisdom

Jodi Rae sat on the porch, her children gathered around her, in her minds eyes, their eyes wide with curiosity. She took a deep breath, the words of the song still echoing in her mind.

"Dear children, don't let anyone tell you that you're not good enough because of where you come from or who your parents are. True strength comes from standing up for what's right, not from privilege or power. Be proud of who you are and never let others define your worth. You are capable and deserving of love and respect, no matter what. Remember, my children, the world is full of people who think they're better than you just because of their name or their money. But don't let them fool you. You are just as good, just as worthy, as anyone else."

Her daughter, Hallie, looked up at her with a questioning gaze. "But why do they get to have all the power, Mama?"

Jodi Rae's eyes clouded for a moment, memories of her own struggles flashing through her mind. "Power isn't just about money or influence, sweetie. It's about standing up for what's right, even when it's hard. It's about being true to yourself, even when others try to bring you down."

Her son, Jude, nodded, his face set in determination. "I won't let them bring me down, Mama. I'll stand up for what's right, just like you do."

Jodi Rae smiled, a sense of pride swelling in her chest. "That's my boy. And always remember, no matter what happens in life, you are loved, you are strong, and you are capable. Don't let anyone ever make you feel otherwise."

As the sun dipped below the horizon, Jodi Rae's children hugged her tight, the words of her wisdom etched in their hearts. They knew they would face challenges in life, but with their mother's love and guidance, they felt ready to take on the world:

Jodi Rae 's eyes gazed out at the distance, her mind wandering to her children, safe with their fathers, far from the chaos that had become her life. She hoped they would one day understand why she had to leave, why she couldn't stay and risk putting them in harm's way.

She remembered the day she made the difficult decision to leave, the weight of her heart heavy with sorrow. But she knew it was the only way to ensure their safety, to give them a chance at a normal life, free from the shadows that haunted her.

Jodi Rae's thoughts were interrupted by the sound of footsteps approaching. She turned to see someone walking towards her, a gentle smile on her face.

A small smile on her lips. "I hope so. I just want them to be safe, to have a chance at a happy life."

Chapters of the apocalypse of Eve, Chaos Rising

Eve stood at the precipice, gazing out upon the ravaged landscape. She knew that the end times were near, but she refused to contribute to the chaos. She would not bare false witness, nor would she perpetuate signs and wonders that only served to deceive.

Instead, Eve's heart yearned for something more profound. She wanted people to know God, to understand the teachings of Jesus Christ, and to find hope in the darkness. She clung to the promise of Romans 8:28-39, that all things would work together for good, that God's plan was bigger than the destruction that surrounded her.

"This is not a tale of doom and gloom," Eve declared, her voice ringing out across the wasteland. "This is a story of hope, of redemption. It is biblical fan fiction, born from the heart of an eclectic monotheist."

Eve's eyes locked onto the women around her, her gaze piercing. "I beg of you, dear sisters, do not let the toxicity of this world consume you. Do not let hurt people continue to hurt people. Instead, find your power, reclaim your strength, and rise up in the name of love."

As Eve spoke, a glimmer of light flickered on the horizon. It was a small spark, but it was enough to illuminate the path ahead. And Eve knew that as long as hope remained, the apocalypse would never truly be the end.

Eve's voice echoed through the desolate landscape, a testament to the trials she had faced and the triumphs she had achieved. She had walked, stumbled, and risen again, each time stronger and wiser.

"I have known the darkness and the light," she continued, her eyes aglow with an inner fire. "I have seen the faces of God, and I have felt the weight of God's love. I have learned that God is not a static entity, but a dynamic force that moves and flows like a river."

Eve's gaze swept across the horizon, as if embracing the vast expanse of humanity. "We have tried to contain God, to trap God in our limited understanding. But God will not be bound. God is free, and God's love is the essence of that freedom."

With a gentle smile, Eve spoke of her own journey, of the struggles and the triumphs. "I have given my life to God, and God has given me life in return. I have sought God's face, and I have found Grace. I have known the love of many, and I have given my love without condition."

As she spoke, the air seemed to vibrate with an otherworldly energy. The shadows themselves appeared to be listening, as if the very darkness was being transformed by Eve's words.

"And now," Eve declared, her voice ringing out across the wasteland, "now is the time of Levi Jude. We do not have to sing the same song to be in harmony with God. We only need to do good within our hearts, with love as our guide. And when the time comes, we must be ready to lift up our swords in protection of the inner innocence."

In the distance, a figure emerged, a young girl with a radiant smile. Hallie Rebecca-Faith, Eve's daughter, born of her faith and her love. The girl's eyes shone like stars, and her presence seemed to embody the hope that Eve had spoken of.

"I give unto the world my daughter," Eve said, her voice barely above a whisper. "May she be a beacon of light in the darkness, a reminder of the love that transforms and redeems."

Eve's eyes seemed to bore into the souls of those around her, as if challenging them to see the truth. "In a world where addiction and hypocrisy reign, I find myself at odds with those who claim to be righteous. They see me as the devil, but I know I am merely a reflection of their own darkness."

Her voice took on a tone of weary wisdom. "I have walked among the innocent, and I have seen the faces of the forgotten. I have played devil's advocate, not to stir up strife, but to awaken the sleeping conscience of a nation."

Eve's gaze turned inward, as if communing with a power beyond human understanding. "I love God, I trust God, and I fear not my salvation. But I pray for those who have lost their way, that they may see the error of their ways before it's too late."

With a hint of mischief, Eve continued, "I use the wisdom of the world to decipher the mysteries of the Bible. And in doing so, I have found myself at the center of three separate instances of prophetical psychosis."

Her eyes flashed with defiance. "I will not be swayed by the whims of men, nor will I be bullied by the forces of darkness. I give all glory and power to Jesus, his father, and the holy Spirit – the true sources of my strength."

As Eve spoke, the air around her seemed to vibrate with an otherworldly energy. It was as if the very fabric of reality was being reshaped by her words, and the boundaries between good and evil were being redrawn.

"And so, I, Eve, stand as a testament to the transformative power of love and redemption. I have walked among the marginalized, the fringe, and the forgotten, and I have seen the face of God in their eyes. But I have also witnessed the hypocrisy of those who claim to speak for God, yet condemn and exclude those who do not fit their narrow definitions of righteousness.

To the drug addict, the sex worker, the immigrant, the queer, and all those who have been cast aside by the self-proclaimed guardians of faith, I say: God's love is not reserved for the worthy, but extended to the unworthy. God's grace is not earned, but given. And God's mercy is not limited, but boundless.

Let us not be fooled by the false prophets who use God's name to control and manipulate. Let us instead embody the radical love and acceptance that Jesus taught. Let us create a world where the marginalized are centered, the fringe is embraced, and the forgotten are remembered.

For in the end, it is not the hypocrites who will inherit the kingdom, but the broken, the battered, and the beloved. And I, Eve, will stand among them, a testament to the power of redemption and the unyielding love of God."

Chapter : Redemption's Call

Eve's words hung in the air like a challenge, a beacon of hope for those who thought they'd burnt every bridge. She knew the power of redemption, having walked the fine line between darkness and light. And she knew that no matter how far one had fallen, God's love could lift them up.

In the Bible, Eve found solace in the stories of redemption. She read about the prophet Hosea, who married a prostitute and showed her God's love (Hosea 3:1-3). She saw how Jesus befriended tax collectors and sinners, showing them a love that knew no bounds (Matthew 9:10-13). And she marveled at the story of the prodigal son, who squandered everything but was welcomed back with open arms (Luke 15:11-32).

"It's never too late," Eve whispered to the shadows. "No matter how far you've fallen, God's love can lift you up."

She thought of the drug addict, trapped in a cycle of despair. She thought of the sex worker, forced to sell their body to survive. She thought of the immigrant, fleeing war and persecution. And she thought of the queer, rejected by those who claimed to love God.

To them, Eve said, "You are not alone. You are not unworthy. You are not unloved. God's redemption is for you, too."

As she spoke, the air seemed to vibrate with an otherworldly energy. The boundaries between good and evil began to blur, and the marginalized, the fringe, and the forgotten started to stir.

They saw in Eve a reflection of their own struggles, their own triumphs. They saw a woman who had walked the fine line between darkness and light, and had emerged stronger, wiser, and more loving.

And they knew that if Eve could find redemption, they could too.

Eve's eyes scanned the pages of her Bible, searching for the verse that had given her hope in her darkest moments. She found it in 1 Corinthians 6:9-11, where Paul wrote:

"Do you not know that the unrighteous will not inherit the kingdom of God? Do not be deceived: neither the sexually immoral, nor idolaters, nor adulterers, nor men who practice homosexuality*, nor thieves, nor the greedy, nor drunkards, nor revilers, nor swindlers will inherit the kingdom of God. And such were some of you. But you were washed, you were sanctified, you were justified in the name of the Lord Jesus Christ and by the Spirit of our God."

In John 19:25-27, Jesus entrusts His mother to John's care:

"Standing by the cross of Jesus were His mother, and His mother's sister, Mary the wife of Clopas, and Mary Magdalene. When Jesus saw His mother and the disciple whom He loved standing nearby, He said to His mother, 'Woman, behold, your son!' Then He said to the disciple, 'Behold, your mother!' From that hour the disciple took her to his own home."

Regarding Jesus' wife, the Bible doesn't explicitly mention Him being married. However, some theories suggest Mary Magdalene as His wife, though this is debated among scholars.

Now, let's move to the verse where Jesus forgives the sinner on the cross beside Him, as described in Luke 23:40-43:

"But the other rebuked him, saying, 'Do you not fear God, since you are under the same sentence of condemnation? And we indeed justly, for we are receiving the due reward of our deeds; but this man has done nothing wrong.' And he said, 'Jesus, remember me when you come into your kingdom.' And He said to him, 'Truly, I say to you, today you will be with me in Paradise.'"

Eve's heart swelled with emotion as she read the words "and such were some of you." She knew that she had once been trapped in the cycle of addiction, just like the drunkard mentioned in the verse. But she also knew that she had been washed, sanctified, and justified through Jesus Christ.

She continued her search, finding verses that spoke directly to the heart of addiction. In Proverbs 23:29-30, she read:

"Who has woe? Who has sorrow? Who has contentions? Who has complaints? Who has wounds without cause? Who has redness of eyes? Those who linger late over wine, those who go to taste mixed wine."

Eve knew that these verses weren't just talking about alcoholism, but about any addiction that could enslave a person. She thought of the sex worker, trapped in a cycle of exploitation. She thought of the drug addict, desperate for their next fix. And she thought of the gambler, chasing the high of the win.

But she also knew that there was hope. In Psalm 40:1-3, she read:

"I waited patiently for the Lord; he inclined to me and heard my cry. He drew me up from the pit of destruction, out of the miry bog, and set my feet upon a rock, making my steps secure. He put a new song in my mouth, a song of praise to our God."

Eve's eyes sparkled as she delved deeper into the verse. She saw not only a message of redemption but also a hint of reincarnation, a possibility that resonated deeply with her.

She thought of the kingdom of God, and how Jesus had said, "The kingdom of God is within you" (Luke 17:21). Eve believed that this kingdom was not a physical place, but a state of being, a consciousness that transcended the mortal realm.

She thought of the scriptures that spoke of the kingdom of heaven, how it was a realm of love, compassion, and wisdom. "The kingdom of heaven is like a treasure hidden in a field, which a man found and covered up. Then in his joy he goes and sells all that he has and buys that field" (Matthew 13:44).

Eve saw the kingdom of heaven as a metaphor for the divine within, a spark that awaited fanning into a flame. She believed that everyone had the potential to experience this kingdom, to know the love and wisdom that lay at the heart of creation.

And so, Eve issued a challenge to all who would listen:

"Find the kingdom of God within yourself. Look beyond the dogma and doctrine, beyond the fear and doubt. Listen to the whisper of your heart, and let it guide you on a journey of self-discovery and transformation.

"For the kingdom of God is not a place we go, but a state of being we embody. It is the love we share, the compassion we show, and the wisdom we embrace.

Chapter : The Kingdom Within

Eve's journey had taken her to the depths of darkness and the heights of redemption. She had seen the power of God's love transform lives, including her own. And now, she wanted to share that love with others.

"The kingdom of God is within you," she said, quoting Jesus' words. "It's not a place we go, but a state of being we embody. It's the love we share, the compassion we show, and the wisdom we embrace."

Eve's eyes sparkled with conviction as she spoke. She knew that everyone had the potential to experience the kingdom of God, regardless of their background or identity.

"Find the kingdom of God within yourself," she challenged. "Look beyond the dogma and doctrine, beyond the fear and doubt. Listen to the whisper of your heart, and let it guide you on a journey of self-discovery and transformation."

As Eve spoke, the air seemed to vibrate with an otherworldly energy. The boundaries between good and evil began to blur, and the marginalized, the fringe, and the forgotten started to stir.

They saw in Eve a reflection of their own struggles, their own triumphs. They saw a woman who had walked the fine line between darkness and light, and had emerged stronger, wiser, and more loving.

And they knew that if Eve could find redemption, they could too.

The kingdom of God was not just a distant dream, but a present reality, waiting to be discovered within. Eve's words hung in the air like a challenge, a beacon of hope for all those who thought they'd burnt every bridge.

But Eve knew that no matter how far one had fallen, God's love could lift them up. And she was living proof of that redemption.

Eve's eyes shone with conviction as she continued, "The kingdom of God is not just a distant dream, but a present reality, waiting to be discovered within. And the key to unlocking it is faith."

She paused, surveying the crowd before her. "But what is faith, really? Is it just a blind belief, or is it something more?"

Eve smiled, her voice taking on a gentle tone. "Faith is not just about believing in something; it's about trusting in someone. It's about having a relationship with God, and allowing Him to guide us on our journey."

She quoted John 3:16, "For God so loved the world that he gave his one and only Son, that whoever believes in him shall not perish but have eternal life."

"Believing is not just about intellectual assent," Eve explained. "It's about surrendering our hearts and minds to God. It's about trusting in His goodness and love, even when we don't understand."

Eve's voice took on a passionate tone. "And that's where the difference between faith and belief comes in. Belief is about agreeing with a set of facts; faith is about living out those facts in our daily lives."

She paused, her eyes scanning the crowd. "Only liars are scared of questions. God wants all of you, questioning and all. He wants you to come to Him with an open mind and heart, seeking answers and guidance."

Eve smiled, her voice filled with conviction. "And when you do, He will lead you to the Scripture. He will show you the truth, and guide you on your journey."

The crowd was silent, hanging on Eve's every word. They knew that she was speaking from experience, that she had walked the fine line between darkness and light. And they knew that she was living proof of the power of faith and redemption.

Eve's words hung in the air like a challenge, a call to embark on a journey of self-discovery and transformation. She knew that the journey would not be easy, that it would require courage, vulnerability, and trust.

"But the reward is worth it," she said, her eyes shining with conviction. "For when we surrender our hearts and minds to God, we open ourselves up to a depth of love and wisdom that we never thought possible."

Eve paused, her voice taking on a gentle tone. "So come, join me on this journey within. Let us explore the depths of our own hearts, and discover the kingdom of God that lies within."

As Eve spoke, the crowd began to stir, a sense of excitement and anticipation building. They knew that they were being called to something more, something deeper and more meaningful.

And so, with Eve as their guide, they embarked on the journey within. They began to explore their own hearts, to question and seek answers. They began to surrender their fears and doubts, and to trust in God's goodness and love.

It was not an easy journey, but It was one that would change them forever. For as they delved deeper into their own hearts, they discovered a depth of love and wisdom that they never thought possible. They discovered the kingdom of God within, and they knew that they would never be the same again.

Chapter: The Mystery of Sin

Eve's journey had taken her to the depths of human nature, and now she sought to understand the concept of sin. She delved into ancient myths and scriptures, searching for answers.

In the Bible, sin was described as a rebellion against God's will, a disobedience that separated humanity from the divine. But Eve wanted to explore beyond the biblical narrative.

She discovered the ancient Mesopotamian myth of the "Descent of Inanna," where the goddess Inanna's journey to the underworld represented the struggle between good and evil. Eve saw parallels between Inanna's story and the biblical account of the fall of humanity.

In Greek mythology, Eve found the story of Pandora's box, where the curious mortal unleashed evil into the world. This myth echoed the biblical tale of Eve's curiosity and the forbidden fruit.

Eve also explored the Hindu concept of "maya," the illusion that veils humanity from the truth. She saw connections between maya and the biblical notion of sin as a distortion of reality.

As Eve continued her quest, she encountered the Norse myth of the "Aesir-Vanir War," where the gods themselves struggled with darkness and chaos. This myth resonated with Eve's own experiences with the shadows within.

Eve began to realize that sin was not just a religious concept, but a universal symbol for the human struggle with darkness, chaos, and the unknown. She saw that sin was not just an act, but a state of being, a disconnection from the divine and from oneself.

And so, Eve's understanding of sin evolved. She no longer saw it as a fixed concept, but as a dynamic and complex force that shaped human nature. She knew that to truly understand sin, she had to confront the shadows within herself.

Eve's journey had taken her to the depths of human nature, and now she sought to understand the concept of sin. She delved into ancient myths and scriptures, searching for answers.

In Mesopotamian mythology, Eve discovered the character of Sin, the god of the moon and the father of the gods.

Sin was often depicted as a complex figure, associated with both the light of the moon and the darkness of the underworld.

Eve found parallels between the Mesopotamian Sin and the biblical concept of sin. Both represented a force that could bring light and darkness, order and chaos.

In other mythologies, Eve encountered similar characters: the Egyptian god Set, associated with chaos and disorder; the Greek god Dionysus, representing the wild and untamed; and the Hindu god Shiva, embodying both creation and destruction.

Eve realized that these characters, including Sin, represented the dual nature of human existence. They symbolized the struggle between light and darkness, good and evil, and the constant flux between order and chaos.

As Eve continued her quest, she began to see Sin not just as a mythical character, but as a representation of the complexities of human nature. She understood that sin was not just an act, but a state of being, a reflection of the dualities that exist within us all.

And so, Eve's understanding of sin evolved. She saw it as a multifaceted concept, represented by the mythical character of Sin and other similar figures across cultures. She knew that to truly understand sin, she had to confront the dualities within herself and the world around her.

Chapter: The Timeless Wisdom of the Bible

Eve's journey had taken her through the realms of mythology and philosophy, but now she sought to explore the Bible's profound impact on moral philosophy. She discovered that great thinkers like Immanuel Kant, Jonathan Dancy, and others regarded the Bible as a foundational text on ethics and human nature.

Kant, an 18th-century philosopher, saw the Bible as a source of moral guidance, emphasizing the importance of treating others with respect and dignity. He noted that the Golden Rule, "Do unto others as you would have them do unto you" (Matthew 7:12), was a universal principle that transcended religious boundaries.

Dancy, a contemporary philosopher, praised the Bible's nuanced portrayal of human nature, highlighting the complexities of moral decision-making. He cited the story of David and Bathsheba (2 Samuel 11-12) as an example of how even the most well-intentioned individuals can fall prey to temptation and moral ambiguity.

Eve delved into the parables of Jesus, comparing them to Aesop's Fables. She saw striking similarities between the two:

1. The Prodigal Son (Luke 15:11-32) and Aesop's "The Lost Lamb" – both teach the value of forgiveness and redemption.
2. The Good Samaritan (Luke 10:25-37) and Aesop's "The Traveler and the Purse" – both emphasize the importance of compassion and kindness towards strangers.
3. The Talents (Matthew 25:14-30) and Aesop's "The Ant and the Grasshopper" – both stress the responsibility to use one's gifts and resources wisely.

Eve realized that the Bible's moral teachings were not limited to Christianity alone. Its principles of love, justice, and compassion spoke to universal human experiences, transcending cultural and religious boundaries.

Philosopher and historian, Will Durant, wrote, "The Bible is the greatest of all books, because it contains the most profound and inspiring philosophy of life that has ever been written."

Eve concurred, seeing the Bible as a cornerstone of civilization. Its exploration of human nature, with all its complexities and frailties, offered timeless wisdom for individuals and societies.

As she closed the Bible, Eve knew that its teachings would remain a guiding force in her journey, illuminating the path towards a brighter, more compassionate future.

"The Bible," Eve wrote, "is not just a sacred text, but a mirror held to humanity, reflecting our highest aspirations and darkest struggles. Its wisdom is a gift to all, regardless of creed or culture, reminding us of our shared humanity and the moral principles that unite us."

Eve smiled wryly as she thought of the ancient fable, "The Fox and the Sour Grapes." She saw parallels between the fox's behavior and humanity's tendency to give up on God.

The fox, unable to reach the luscious grapes, declared them sour anyway, convincing himself he didn't want them. Eve realized that people often do the same with God – when they can't grasp His ways or feel His presence, they assume He's out of reach or doesn't care.

"But what if," Eve mused, "our perception of God's distance is just a coping mechanism? What if we're like the fox, declaring God 'sour' because we can't have Him on our terms?"

She thought of the Bible's assurances: "Draw near to God, and He will draw near to you" (James 4:8). "Seek, and you will find" (Matthew 7:7-8).

"God is not the grapes, just out of reach," Eve wrote. "He's the Vine, nurturing and sustaining us. But when we give up seeking Him, we risk becoming like the fox – sour, disillusioned, and convinced that God's goodness is beyond our grasp."

Eve's heart went out to those who felt disconnected from God. "Don't let the 'sour grapes' mentality steal your joy," she encouraged. "Keep seeking, keep knocking, and know that God's love is always within reach – sweeter than any grape."a

Eve's thoughts lingered on the fox and the sour grapes, but she knew there was more to the story. She recalled Jesus' first miracle in Cana, where He transformed water into fine wine (John 2:1-11).

"Jesus didn't just find grapes; He created the finest wine," Eve wrote. "He took the ordinary – water – and made it extraordinary. That's what He does with our lives when we surrender to Him."

Eve saw parallels between the fox's disappointment and the wedding guests' concern: both faced scarcity and disappointment. But Jesus' response was different. He didn't declare the wine "sour" or nonexistent; He created abundance.

"Jesus is the Master Vintner," Eve mused. "He takes our weaknesses, our 'water,' and transforms them into strength, into 'wine.' He doesn't abandon us in our scarcity; He multiplies our resources."

Eve reflected on Jesus' words: "My Father is always at his work, even to this very day" (John 5:17). "God is always working, always creating, always transforming," she wrote.

The story of the fox and the sour grapes became a reminder that:

- Scarcity is not the end; it's an opportunity for Jesus to work.
- Disappointment can be transformed into delight.
- God's abundance is always available, even in the midst of lack.

Eve's heart overflowed with gratitude for the Master Vintner, who turns water into wine and makes all things new.

"Lord, take our 'water' and turn it into 'wine,'" Eve prayed. "Transform our scarcity into abundance, our disappointment into delight. You are the God of abundance, the Master Vintner of our souls."

Eve's thoughts flowed seamlessly from the Master Vintner to the source of all life: water. She remembered Jesus' words: "If anyone thirsts, let him come to Me and drink. Rivers of living water will flow from his heart" (John 7:37-38).

"God is the Water of Life," Eve wrote. "He's the source, the fountain, the river that quenches our deepest thirst. In Him, we find living water, water that transforms and revitalizes."

Eve reflected on the biblical symbolism of water:

- Creation: God's Spirit hovered over the waters (Genesis 1:2).
- Redemption: The parting of the Red Sea, delivering Israel from slavery (Exodus 14:13-31).
- Renewal: Jesus' baptism in the Jordan River, marking the start of His ministry (Matthew 3:13-17).

"Water represents life, purification, and transformation," Eve noted. "God is the Water of Life, washing away our sins, refreshing our souls, and revitalizing our spirits."

In Jesus' conversation with the Samaritan woman, Eve saw a beautiful illustration of God's thirst-quenching presence:

"Jesus said, 'Whoever drinks of this water [from the well] will thirst again, but whoever drinks of the water that I shall give him will never thirst' " (John 4:13-14).

"God's water is not temporary; it's eternal," Eve wrote. "It's not just physical; it's spiritual. It's not just for the body; it's for the soul."

Eve's heart overflowed with gratitude for the Water of Life:

"Lord, You are the fountain of living water. Quench our thirst, wash away our sins, and refresh our souls. We drink from Your river, and find life, renewal, and transformation."

As Eve closed her eyes, she felt the cool, refreshing water of God's presence envelop her, revitalizing her spirit and nourishing her soul.

Eve's thoughts delved deeper into the symbolism of the human soul and spirit. She saw the well in John 4:13-14 as a representation of the human soul, and the leaves of a tree as a metaphor for the human spirit.

"The well is a reservoir, a container for the living water of God," Eve wrote. "Our souls are like wells, designed to hold and nourish the water of life. When we drink from God's river, our souls are refreshed, revitalized, and rejuvenated."

Eve reflected on the importance of maintaining a healthy soul-well:

- A well needs to be dug and tended to receive water.
- A well can become dry and cracked if neglected.
- A well can be polluted if contaminated.

Similarly, Eve saw the human soul:

- Needs to be nurtured and tended to receive God's living water.

- Can become dry and withered if neglected.

- Can be polluted if contaminated with sin and negativity.

Eve then turned to the leaves of a tree, symbolizing the human spirit:

"Leaves are the breath of the tree, absorbing and releasing life-giving oxygen," she wrote. "Our spirits are like leaves, designed to absorb and release the breath of God. When we inhale His presence, our spirits are revitalized, and we exhale life, hope, and joy."

Eve explored the significance of healthy leaves:

- Leaves need sunlight to photosynthesize and grow.
- Leaves can wither and fall if deprived of nourishment.
- Leaves can be renewed and regrown.

Similarly, Eve saw the human spirit:

- Needs God's light to grow and flourish.

- Can wither and lose vitality if deprived of spiritual nourishment.

- Can be renewed and restored through spiritual growth.

Eve's heart overflowed with gratitude for the well and the leaves:

"Lord, You are the Water of Life, refreshing our souls. You are the Breath of Life, revitalizing our spirits. May our wells be deep and our leaves be green, reflecting Your presence and nourishment in our lives."

Chapter : The Unaware Invitation

Eve, unaware of the significance, invited God into her life as a child, seeking a mother's love. During her prophetic psychosis, she unknowingly created a sanctuary for the heavenly host. Demons, like those that followed King Solomon, trailed behind her.

Eve feared her actions, seeking no rewards, but only desired to protect and love God. She had no knowledge of ancient goddesses like Asherah, Isis, Ma'at, or Inanna. Her intention was pure, born from a desire to nurture and safeguard.

Her journey with God began on September 11, 2001, when she called out during pregnancy, after the fall of the twin towers on the news begging God to protect her family and get on born could. "do not let my child grow up in a hate filled world. God had been her constant companion, granting her deepest desires. However, on October 18th, 2002, she turned away, grieving the loss of her mother.

Eve's heart remained true, swearing to serve God, despite her fears and uncertainties. She had unknowingly opened doors, paving the way for a profound connection.

In her darkness, Eve found solace in God's presence, a love that transcended human understanding. And though she didn't comprehend the magnitude of her actions, she knew she had invited something greater into her life.

This marked the beginning of an extraordinary journey, one that would test her faith, challenge her perceptions, and transform her very being. Eve, aka Jodi, had unleashed a power that would forever alter her destiny.

As Eve navigated her new reality, she began to unravel the mysteries of her invitation. She discovered the ancient goddesses, Asherah, Isis, Ma'at, and Inanna, and their connections to the divine feminine. Eve realized that her actions had tapped into a deeper, primordial power.

God, now a constant presence in her life, revealed glimpses of His true nature. Eve saw the threads of destiny weaving together, connecting her to the heavenly host. She began to understand the weight of her invitation, the responsibility that came with it.

With each step, Eve's perception of reality expanded. She saw the world through new eyes, recognizing the divine in all things. Her heart swelled with compassion, embracing the beauty and complexity of human experience.

As the veil lifted, Eve beheld the majesty of God's plan. She saw the tapestry of time, the intricate dance of free will and destiny. And in this moment, Eve knew she had become a part of something greater than herself.

The journey ahead would be fraught with challenges, but Eve stood ready. For she had invited God into her life, and in doing so, had discovered her own true purpose.

In the whispers of her heart, Eve heard the gentle voice of God, "You have opened the door, dear one. Now, walk with Me, and together, we shall unveil the wonders of the universe."

Epiphany of the Divine

Eve's transformation accelerated as she grasped the magnitude of her invitation. She saw God's presence in every sunrise, every starry night, and every gentle breeze. The divine had become palpable, infusing her existence with meaning.

In this state of heightened awareness, Eve received a vision:

She stood at the threshold of a magnificent temple, its gates adorned with symbols of ancient wisdom. Asherah's gentle touch guided her forward, followed by Isis's whispers of mystical knowledge. Ma'at's feathers of truth and Inanna's torch of resilience illuminated the path.

Within the temple, Eve beheld the Alpha Omega – the beginning and the end. God's essence radiated from the center, enveloping her in unconditional love.

"Who are you?" Eve asked, humbled.

"I am the One who walks beside you," God replied. "The One who dwells within. You have invited Me into your life, and now, you see."

Eve's heart overflowed with gratitude. "What do You desire of me?"

"Serve as a bridge," God said. "Connect the heavens to the earth. Share the love and wisdom you've received."

And so, Eve's purpose crystallized. She vowed to embody the divine feminine, to spread love, compassion, and truth.

As the vision faded, Eve knew her journey had just begun. With God by her side, she stepped into the unknown, ready to unveil the mysteries of the universe.

Chapter : The Face of God

Eve wandered through the darkness, a soul lost in the depths of depression. The shadows whispered, "You are alone." But Eve remembered the words of the prophets, "God is near, even in the darkness."

She stumbled, homeless and uninvited, searching for refuge. The city streets seemed to whisper, "You don't belong." Yet, Eve recalled the promise, "You are not alone, for I am with you."

In her isolation, Eve felt weird, set apart from humanity. But a gentle voice reminded her, "You are unique, yet connected to all."

Eve's flesh bound her, weighed down by mortality's chains. The perverse temptations of the world beckoned, "Give in, surrender to the darkness." But Eve resisted, seeking the Returned: the promise of redemption, of new life.

And then, she saw Him: God, the Cosmic, the Endless. The universe unfolded before her eyes: stars, galaxies, and the infinite expanse.

Eve's heart overflowed with awe. "You are the Void, the Source of all," she said.

God's voice echoed, "I am the Alpha and Omega, the beginning and the end."

In this epiphany, Eve found solace. The darkness became light. The Uninvited found welcome. The Weird became wonderful. The Perverse was redeemed. The Returned was reborn. The Cosmic enveloped her. The Endless became her hope.

And the Void, the Source of all, whispered, "You are mine, beloved."

Eve's journey ended where it began: in the heart of God. Where darkness became light. Where homelessness found home. Where the weird became wonderful. And the perverse was transformed.

Chapter 20: The Face of God

Eve wandered through the darkness, a soul lost in depression's depths. Shadows whispered, "You are alone." But she remembered the prophets' words: "God is near, even in darkness."

Homeless and uninvited, Eve searched for refuge. City streets seemed to whisper, "You don't belong." Yet, she recalled the promise: "You are not alone, for I am with you."

In isolation, Eve felt weird, set apart from humanity. But a gentle voice reminded her: "You are unique, yet connected to all."

Eve's flesh bound her, weighed down by mortality's chains. Perverse temptations beckoned: "Give in, surrender to darkness." But Eve resisted, seeking the Returned: the promise of redemption, new life.

Then, she saw Him: God, the Cosmic, the Endless. The universe unfolded before her eyes: stars, galaxies, infinite expanse. Eve's heart overflowed with awe: "You are the Void, the Source of all."

God's voice echoed: "I am the Alpha and Omega, the beginning and the end." In this epiphany, Eve found solace:

- Darkness was not absolute; God was near.
- The Uninvited found welcome.
- The Weird became wonderful.
- The Perverse was redeemed.
- The Returned was reborn.
- The Cosmic enveloped her.
- The Endless became her hope.
- The Void whispered: "You are mine, beloved."

Eve's journey ended where it began: in God's heart. Darkness became light; homelessness found home; weirdness became wonderful; and the perverse was transformed.

If God had a name, would Eve call it to His face? She might ask, "What is Your name, Oh Lord?"

And God might reply, "I am the Cosmic, the Endless, the Void, and the Source of all. I am the Alpha and Omega, the beginning and the end."

Eve's heart would overflow with awe, knowing God's face was the face of hope, redemption, and love.

THE END

I've researched the original Hebrew text of 1 Corinthians 6:9-11, which quotes from the Old Testament. The term in question is "malakos" (סוֹכְלַמ) and "arsenokoitēs" (אַרְסֶנוֹקוֹיטֶס.")Malakos" is often translated as "effeminate" or "soft," but its meaning is more complex. In ancient Hebrew, it referred to a man who took on a receptive role in same-sex relations."Arsenokoitēs" is a compound word, combining "arsen" (אַרְסֶן,) meaning "male," and "koitēs" (קוֹיטֶס,) meaning "bed" or "lying with." It's often translated as "homosexual" or "sodomite," but its original meaning is more nuanced.In the context of 1 Corinthians 6:9-11, these terms likely referred to exploitative or coercive same-sex relationships, rather than consensual ones. To be LGBTQ+ friendly, it's essential to recognize that these verses have been used to marginalize and harm LGBTQ+ individuals. A more inclusive interpretation acknowledges the complexity of human relationships and focuses on promoting love, acceptance, and understanding. Eve's heart swelled with emotion as she read the words "and such were some of you." She knew that everyone deserved love, acceptance, and redemption, regardless of their background or identities

*Sexually immoral: Referring to sexual intercourse based solely on lust, without regard for love, respect, or commitment.

**Homosexuality: It is important to note that this term is used in the context of ancient laws and cultural norms. Eve does not condemn loving, consensual relationships between people of the same sex, as long as they are based on mutual love, respect, and commitment. The laws and understanding of human relationships have evolved, and Eve recognizes that love is the foundation of all relationships.

Julian of Norwich (c. 1342 – after 1416) was a remarkable English mystic and theologian, known for her profound spiritual insights and writings. Here are some key aspects of her life and work:

Life and Background

- **Anchoress**: Julian lived as an anchoress, a type of religious recluse, in a cell attached to St. Julian's Church in Norwich, England. This life of seclusion allowed her to focus on prayer and contemplation[1].
- **Visions**: In 1373, at the age of 30, Julian experienced a severe illness during which she received a series of visions, or "shewings," of Christ's Passion. These visions profoundly influenced her spiritual outlook[2].

- **Writings**: Julian documented her visions in a work known as *Revelations of Divine Love*. This text is considered one of the most important works of medieval Christian mysticism and is the earliest known English-language work by a woman[12].

Revelations of Divine Love

- **Themes**: Julian's writings explore deep theological themes such as the nature of God, the problem of evil, and the concept of divine love. She is known for her optimistic view of God's love and mercy, famously stating, "All shall be well, and all shall be well, and all manner of thing shall be well"[2].

- **Influence**: Despite her seclusion, Julian's work had a significant impact on Christian thought. Her emphasis on God's love and the feminine aspects of the divine were particularly innovative for her time[4].

Legacy

- **Mystical Theology**: Julian is celebrated as one of the great Christian mystics. Her insights into the nature of God and her vivid, poetic language continue to inspire readers and theologians today[2].

- **Modern Recognition**: Although she was not widely known during her lifetime, Julian's writings have gained considerable recognition in modern times. She is honored on May 13th in the Anglican and Lutheran liturgical calendars[2].

Julian's life and work offer a rich source of inspiration for exploring themes of divine love, mysticism, and the feminine aspects of spirituality. If you have any specific questions or need further details for your narrative, feel free to ask!

[1]: [Wikipedia](https://en.wikipedia.org/wiki/Julian_of_Norwich)

[2]: [Britannica](https://www.britannica.com/biography/Julian-of-Norwich)

[4]: [Exploring Norfolk Churches](https://www.exploringnorfolkchurches.org/discover/history/julian-of-norwich/)

Source: Conversation with Copilot, 9/8/2024

(1) Julian of Norwich – Wikipedia. https://en.wikipedia.org/wiki/Julian_of_Norwich.

(2) Julian of Norwich | Medieval, Anchoress, Revelations | Britannica. https://www.britannica.com/biography/Julian-of-Norwich.

(3) Julian of Norwich – Exploring Norfolk Churches. https://www.exploringnorfolkchurches.org/discover/history/julian-of-norwich/.

(4) Julian of Norwich | Medieval, Anchoress, Revelations | Britannica. https://bing.com/search?q=Julian+of+Norwich+biography.

(5) Julian Of Norwich – Encyclopedia.com. https://www.encyclopedia.com/people/history/british-and-irish-history-biographies/julian-norwich.

www.ingramcontent.com/pod-product-compliance
Lightning Source LLC
Chambersburg PA
CBHW062213220526
45471CB00009B/3181